River Warrior

Fighting to Protect the World's Rivers

For all the River Warriors across the planet who've been bullied, harassed, harmed, or worse. Stand proud and tall, brothers and sisters, and keep fighting!

RIVER WARRIOR

Fighting to Protect the World's Rivers!

By Gary Wockner

Wolverine Farm Publishing

WOLVERINE FARM

Published by Wolverine Farm Publishing, a 501(c)3 non-profit literary/arts organization based in Fort Collins, Colorado. Wolverine Farm Publishing publishes books and newspapers, runs a bookstore inside The Bean Cycle Coffee Shop, operates a Letterpress & Publick House, and hosts/organizes community events and projects.

Wolverine Farm Publishing Mission: To publish quality literature and art that mindfully engages humans with the world.

316 Willow Street, Fort Collins, CO 80524
www. WolverineFarm.org

Cover Design: Gary Wockner

Cover Photo: Wade Graham

ISBN 978-1-937896-11-9

Thank You!

I's so dam lucky! I write, speak, travel, and advocate constantly to fight dams and save rivers! It's great, humbling, and important work. I've gotten to do this because a lot of people have allowed me to be the voice for their river, organization, or company, and they've supported me in so doing. I get to be a megaphone, and these are many of the people I have to thank.

Mark Easter – who got me into this and has stayed in the foxhole from day one, fellow River Warrior!

Kim Jordan, Jenn Vervier, Bryan Simpson, Katie Wallace, Kari Fletcher, Adrian Glasenapp, Christine Perich, Jeff Lebesch and the whole team at New Belgium Brewing – you supported me from the get-go and that made a huge difference.

Hans Cole and the whole crew at Patagonia. The great folks at Clif Bar.

Terry Odendahl and her team at Global Greengrants Fund.

The Save The Poudre team including John Bartholow, Greg Speer, Gina Janett, Todd Simmons, Cordelia Stone, David Roy, Barry Noon, Doug Swartz, and all of the amazing volunteers.

The Save The Colorado team including Dan Beard, John Fielder, Sara Aminzadeh, Mark Dubois, Doug Pflugh, McCrystie Adams, and Mike Chiropolos.

A bunch of people at the Waterkeeper Alliance including Robert F. Kennedy, Jr, Mary Beth Postman, Marc Yaggi, Pete Nichols, Lesley Adams, and lots more.

And more – you know what you are doing (or did) and why it matters: Cat Ebeling, Jennie Curtis, George Wendt, John Kefalas, Randy Fischer, Bob Bacon, Kelly Ohlson, Lisa Poppaw, Stefanie Spear, Betsy Marston, Laura Pritchett, Ben Manvel, Will Walters, the team at International Rivers, Rich Ingebretsen, Jake Williams, Jennifer Sunderland, Alexandra Cousteau, Jill Tidman and the team at the Redford Center, Clark Wockner (River Warrior!), Dan Bihn, Phil Cafaro, Ross Cunniff, Bob Overbeck, James Thompson, Joann Ginal, Kathy Aterno, Elise and Suzanne Jones, Andrew Currie, John Stokes, Darin Atteberry and the City of Fort Collins river team, Matt Rice, Bart Miller, Jon Waterman, Pete McBride, Chris Garre, Jay Kenney, Kristin Stephens, Caroline Wockner, Julia Wockner, Katie Hoffner, Jen Pelz, John Weisheit, Joel Dyer, Wade Graham, Jeni Arndt, Matt Stoecker, and more!

Contents

Introduction

I love fighting dams and saving rivers!

Why?

Maybe it's because whenever I'm boating through big rapids I start laughing out loud so much so that the waves often splash across my face causing me to inhale water while laughing and choking. Maybe it's because I grew up along a river, running wild all day and night, and like a river I believe people and water should flow free and wild. Maybe it's because I've seen children and adults have life-changing experiences along rivers – playing, swimming, rowing, camping, adventuring, unplugged alive and outdoors. Maybe it's because I love the way rivers look, taste, and smell.

This book, *River Warrior*, is a selection of my writings over the last few years. These pieces were all published elsewhere – in books, magazines, newspapers, online news sites, and blogs. I suggest that you don't read this book front to back, but rather pick and wander through it. Just let it take you downstream however you want. Some pieces are short columns that appeared in newspapers, and others are longer essays or photo-essays that appeared in magazines and online news sites. Together, they represent one passionate, dedicated statement – we need to stop damming rivers and start saving them!

The first section, "Saving The World's Rivers," highlights my most recent writing from Peru, Thailand, Spain, Belize, Mexico, Columbia, and Costa Rica. The section also includes a few pieces that wander all over the planet, discussing the problem of dams and climate change, and how the first is making the second worse. In 2014, I started working with Global Greengrants Fund (based in Boulder, CO), and started volunteering for International Rivers (based in Berkeley, CA) as well as the international Waterkeeper Alliance (based in New York City). Those amazing friends and connections have taken me on a tour of a few amazing rivers on the planet and the most dedicated and passionate people who are working to protect those rivers and waterways.

The second section, "Saving The Colorado River," highlights my work over the last seven years as I launched and directed the Save The Colorado River Campaign. Never has a river been so dammed, diverted, and drained as the Colorado – a foolish history and technology that created it that is now being transported across the planet to dam, drain, and destroy rivers everywhere. My good friends at New Belgium Brewing co-founded this adventure with me, and after five years I spun "Save The Colorado" off to be a free-standing 501c3 organization. My board and I are deeply immersed in fighting even more dams on the Colorado River and doing our level best to protect and restore the river for future generations.

The third section, "Saving The Cache la Poudre River," is where my inner River Warrior really took hold. As of this writing (Sept. 2016), we've been fighting for 13 years against a proposed dam that would further drain and destroy the Poudre – this fight has helped me find my own voice, passion, and mission, and we will continue to fight for as long as it takes! I co-founded "Save The Poudre" with the most amazing bunch of colleagues in Fort Collins, CO, and I've had the true privilege of being the leader and spokesperson for this organization. We are standing on the shoulders of a couple generations of Poudre River savers, and we are committed to stopping new dams and protecting the river.

I know this sounds gloomy, but the rivers of the planet are facing an apocalypse of dams. As of this writing, several hundred dams are under construction across the planet, and thousands more are in the planning stages. Rivers are the veins of the earth – providing the life-blood that circulates the nutrition from the air, to the land, to the river, to the ocean, and back to the air. Dams block that circle of life. Dams are like an arterial blockage in the human body, stopping the flow of blood that keeps a person alive. A dam on a river is like a stroke in a person's body. Dams stop the flow of water that we all – including all of those amazing non-human critters and ecosystems – depend on for survival.

What can we do about all of those damn dams? Fight them! Join me in fighting dams and saving rivers! Pick any reason or story or place or river in this book – they all need help. Or, even better, pick your own reason to stand up and fight for your own river. There's plenty of work and rivers to go around.

If I can do it, so can you – River Warriors all!

Gary Wockner
Sept 30, 2016
Fort Collins, CO

Part I: Saving The World's Rivers

Don't Dam The Grand Canyon of Peru!

(*Canoe and Kayak Magazine*, July 2016)

The headwaters and biggest tributary to the Amazon River is facing massive dam threats, but nothing has been built yet and the timing is right to ramp up the campaign to save the Maranon River!

"I believe all rivers are sacred." – Bruno Monteferri, standing at the site of the proposed Chadin II Dam, is Director of Conservamos por Naturaleza and the Maranon River Waterkeeper

Our first wisp of the Maranon River came when we were 6,000 feet above it. We had just driven from the town of Celendin up to the lip of the canyon, and then looked down a couple miles along the steep cliff. The thin chalky-blue line of the Maranon slithered through the bottom of the canyon. A collective "WOW" came from the mouths of the 12 people in our minibus – the canyon was deep, immense, and the river looked like a tiny thread below. Two hours later, after having driven down the snaky one-lane road switch-backing endlessly downward, we arrived at the river in the tiny village of Balsas. A 6-night trip awaited us, during which we would learn about the threats of hydroelectric dams on this beautiful and pristine river.

Six thousand feet below, the Maranon River Canyon is deeper than the Grand Canyon and collects all the water that flows off the east slope of the Andes Mountains in Peru.

They call it "The Grand Canyon of Peru," or sometimes "The Grand Canyon of South America." It drains the entire Peruvian portion of the east slope of the Andes Mountains and is the headwaters and the largest tributary to the Amazon River. As our minibus unloaded, we gawked at the amazing scenery and stumbled around on the cobbled rocks at water's edge. After a couple hours unpacking the trucks and packing up the dry bags, we slipped into the water with four rafts and three kayaks. Our guides were seasoned Peruvian rafters and adventure travelers, and our hosts were the new "Maranon River Waterkeeper" organization which is an affiliate of the international Waterkeeper Alliance.

"The Maranon is a beautiful river – we need your help to save it." -- Leonardo Gonzalez, trip leader and renowned Peruvian adventure traveler who hosted a TV show for five years highlighting extraordinary outdoor trips throughout the country.

Peru has amazing mountains and rivers and provides whitewater adventure opportunities for hundreds-of-thousands of international rafters and kayakers every year. The Maranon River currently has almost no commercial rafting activity on it, and so on our seven-day trip we saw zero other rafters and kayakers. The river offers Class I, II, III, and IV rafting in the dry season in June. The weather was exceptionally dry prior to our arrival, with flow at about 6,000 cubic feet/second (cfs). In the rainy season in March and April the river can swell to over 30,000 cfs and is considered to be un-runnable. Being an undammed Andes mountain river, the Maranon is ecologically pristine with massive sand bars, sediment-filled tributaries, driftwood on the banks, migrating fish and wildlife, and little human activity.

However, the hydroelectric dam-building corporations have had their eyes on this pristine river for decades.

Proposed dam sites on the Maranon River. Image: Sierra Rios

Of the twenty dam sites that have been identified on the Maranon over the last three decades, seven are serious proposals, and four are in the permitting process with the Peruvian government. At least three hydroelectric corporations are proposing the different dams. On the third day of our trip, we paddled through the "Chadin II" dam site, a proposal that has been put forward by the Odebrecht Corporation, a multi-national construction conglomerate based in Brazil. Some good news about this particular dam proposal is that Odebrecht is embroiled in a massive corruption scandal that has put its CEO in prison and has forced the company to stall many of its efforts and eliminate some of its operations, including for the time being, the Chadin II dam proposal. The proposed Chadin II dam would be over 500 feet high and drown dozens of miles of the river canyon including the small vilage of Mendan.

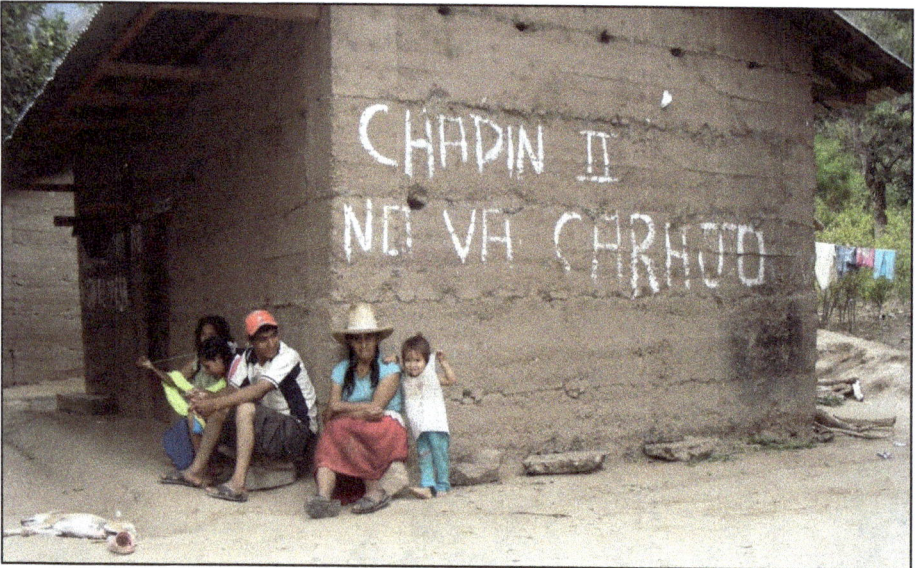

The Chadin II dam site would flood the small farming village of Mendan. Villagers have emblazened anti-dam graffiti across many of their homes.

The last ten years have seen an incresingly contested debate about dams and hydroelectricity in Peru. While the hydroelectric corporations and some factions of the government argue that more electricity is needed, the facts appear to be different. Peru currently meets all of its electric needs with its present system, and the arguments for more electricity are being pushed by the multi-national hydroelectric corporations that hope to sell the electricty – for their corporate profit – to neighboring countries or to the mining industry.

Anti-dam activists also argue that the hydroelectric corporations are running roughshod over the permitting process and the political process surrounding it.

The corporations have been accused of paying off local villagers, paying people to attend public meetings to speak in support of the dams, trespassing on private land in the villages, and creating a hostile situation where villagers and dam opponents are increasingly harrassed and threatened when they speak out. Importantly, anti-dam activists argue that if Peru really needs more electricity, it should focus on wind and solar, instead of damming and destroying its wild and pristine rivers like the Maranon.

"Protecting this river should be a part of the national pride of Peru." – Enrique Ortiz, Program Director, Andes Amazon Fund

The battle to protect the Maranon River has been alive for several years, mostly due to the work and funding of International Rivers and one their grantees, Sierra Rios. Most recently, the newly launched Maranon River Waterkeeper is developing a complementary campaign to fill in some blanks in the campaign plan. Much work needs to be done – legal, financial, research, education and advocacy, international media outreach, and organizing the Peruvian people – so there's plenty of opportunity to engage on many levels to protect the river.

One of the biggest needs of the campaign is to get more attention for the river in media and in funding circles. To achieve that, the Maranon River

Waterkeeper has joined with a Lima-based adventure travel company to launch the "Maranon Experience," which offers a variety of raft trips down the river that can be customized to fit the needs of media, guests, funders, and policymakers. Additional work that is a high priority involves engaging with the Peruvian government on behalf of the river and the Peruvian people. As one of our trip-mates, Enrique Ortiz, noted on our trip:

"Peru needs to have a plan. Right now the hydroelectric corporations have a plan, but Peru doesn't have a plan for the benefit of the environment and the people of Peru."

In support of this planning, several outreach efforts are ongoing and more will begin soon, including an action alert on the Waterkeeper's website that reaches out to the Peruvian government asking the Minister of the Environment to launch a "Strategic Environmental Assessment" that would halt the dams and protect the river while a planning process moves forward.

The Andes rise in the background around every turn along the Maranon River.

Another of the exicting opportunities to protect the Maranon River and the landscape surrounding it involves creating a "National Protected Area" that encompasses both sides of the river. The proposal being pushed forward by regional conservation organizations would protect about 250,000 acres – 175,000 on the western side of the river in the province of Cajamarcas, and 75,000 acres on the eastern side of the river in the provice of Amazonos. While the proposal would not specifically stop the dams, it could create a 'regional conservation area' and potentially become a new eco-tourist zone in Peru to highlight the biodiversity, river, waterfalls, wildlife, Inca ruins, and adventure-travel opportunities. Most tourists who visit Peru head south, towards Machu Piccu. This new northern National Protected Area would help bring a recreational economy and public attention that could help stop the dams and protect the river.

"I think we're in a moment in history where humans really have to change the way we're living on the planet." – Bruno Monteferri, on video

In the last five years, activists and conservation groups are making a bigger commitment to the protection of the Maranon. Accompanying us on our trip was a photographer from World Wildlife Fund which is creating a campaign to support Maranon protection. Funding organizations including Global Greengrants Fund have stepped in to support International Rivers' campaigns and actions. Peruvian organizations including Forum Solidaridad and Ecodess have engaged. Earthrights International and other legal firms are helping to address and support the rights of activists and landowners, as well as the enforcement of Peruvian environmental laws in Peruvian and Latin American courts. In addition, the Wildlife Conservation Society has been engaged in wildlife studies in and along the river that can help support the science to argue against dams being built.

The battle is being fought on multiple fronts. For example, during our raft trip, Bruno Monteferri told our group, "I believe all rivers are sacred. But, we need to tell an economic and a political story too." Likewise, Enrique Ortiz focused on the biological diversity as well as the cultural symbolizm of the river when he told us, "This area should become a national priority for protecting biodiversity, and protecting this river should be a part of the national pride of Peru."

The Maranon offers peace and solitude amidst the massive mountains. Cat Ebeling, afternoon yoga at Magdalena Beach.

As we near the end of our trip and approach the village of Pueblo Malleta, the river begins to widen out with more sand and gravel bars spreading out the flow of water. Along the bends of the river, oasis spring up where farmers have planted small fields including palm trees with coconuts hanging on the branches. We hear and see a few irrigation sprinklers that suck water out of the river and spray fields of mangos and coca. Pueblo Malleta is also the end of much of the mountain-canyon portion of the Maranon. Downstream, the river slips into the Amazon jungle and serves more farming villages, but is also threatened by proposed hydroelectric dams that would stair-step all the way to the Amazon River.

The good news about the Maranon is that no dams have yet been built, and thus the timing is good to increase pressure on the dam-building corporations and the Peruvian government. Additionally, at the same time that the dam companies are stalling their efforts, the mining companies – and their need for electricity – are also slowing down due to the drop in copper prices. Furthermore, the regional governments that straddle the river – Cajamarcas and Amazonas – have diverse opinions about the dams, with opposition increasing as more people are educated and organized. Finally, Peru's adventure travel economy is increasing, and the Maranon is a pritine resource for rafting experiences.

We believe victory is possible – we can save the Maranon!

Resources:
Book a raft trip – visit the Maranon Experience website:
http://maranonexperience.com/
Take action to reach out to the government – visit Maranon River Waterkeeper website: http://maranonwaterkeeper.org/

--end--

THE MEKONG RIVER IS NOT FOR SALE!

(*New Internationalist* and *Boulder Weekly*, May 2016)

"Preserving 'local knowledge' is different than westernized 'nature protection.' We are protecting people's habitats, their homes, lives, food, and voices. This is my home; these are my people," says Mr. Chak Kineesee, Program and Outreach Director at the Mekong School for Local Knowledge, as he guides us on a longboat ride up the river.

Mr. Chak was born in a village east of the Mekong River and is a member of one of the Hill Tribes of Northern Thailand. He works to protect the river and the livelihoods of the local indigenous people. Mr. Chak gave us a tour of one of the village forestry programs as well as a longboat ride up the Mekong River.

Dawn breaks hot and smoky on the Mekong River in Chiang Khong, Thailand on April 11, 2016. Looking across the river to the neighboring Laos town of Huay Xai, the sun eases above the hills amidst intense haze and humidity. April is the hottest month in Thailand, and April 2016 was the hottest month in 65 years, breaking 100 degrees Fahrenheit every day in the entire month. The dawn smoke is from slash-and-burn agriculture that is causing havoc on the forests on the Laos side of the border and throughout northern Thailand.

We start our day by meeting at the Mekong School for Local Knowledge which sits along the banks of the Mekong River in the small town of Chiang Khong in the very north of the Thailand several kilometers downstream from the Golden Triangle where Burma, Thailand, and Laos meet on the river. The School is a very small NGO and a grantee of Global Greengrants Fund (GGF) and GGF's partner International Rivers. The School uses the phrase "local knowledge" in the same way that we think of "indigenous knowledge" – that which has developed naturally as a part of the lives of native peoples.

China has built several dams upstream on the river that impact the lives of downstream residents here in Chiang Khong. Many more dams are proposed on the Mekong River in China, down through Thailand, and downstream through Viet Nam and Cambodia. The river – and the local indigenous people and their livelihood – is severely threatened by dams that change the flow in the river, drown fish and bird habitat, drown villages and displace people, and submerge and erase local centuries-old knowledge of how to live sustainably on the landscape.

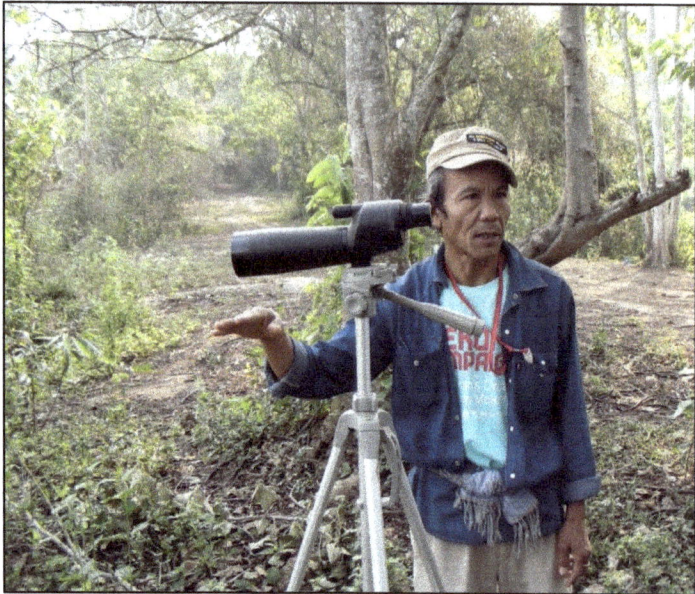

"When the birds come, the fish come," explains Mr. Chak who keeps close track of bird migrations throughout the river's ecosystem. "And that is when our people also come to sustainably harvest the fish."

We visited in April during the dry season and first took a tour of the nearby forest preserve and the Ing River – which is a very small tributary to the Mekong River a few kilometers southeast of Chiang Khong – where local people fish and gather food. Where Mr. Chak is standing right now would be under 2 meters of water when it floods in the wet season. But here's the problem – the upstream Chinese dams hold back some of the water and divert it out during the wet season, and so the floods no longer occur as high and often as they did in the past. The landscape – and the local peoples' livelihood – have irrevocably changed. Birds don't have as much nesting habitat. Fish can't spawn as readily as they did before the dams. Local people can't gather the forage, crops, and fish from the native landscape as much as in the past.

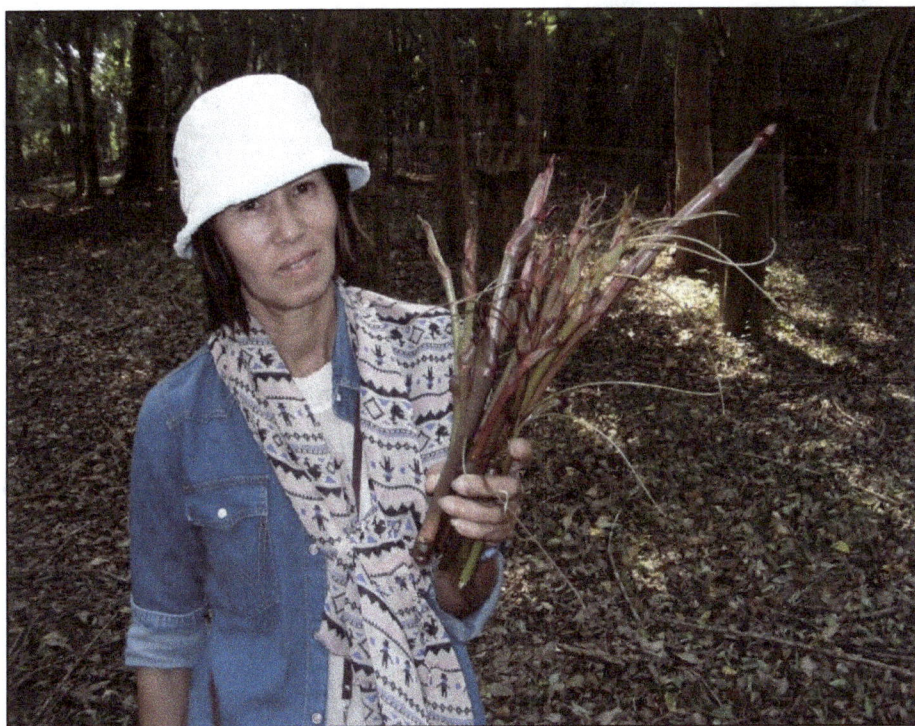

Mrs. Yod La is a member of the Dai Yaun tribe which is the oldest Hill Tribe in the area. She joined us on our tour of the forest preserve near the Ing River. While we walked and drove through the forest, she harvested wild vegetables from the forest floor. If the forest no longer floods because of the upstream dams, the food will no longer grow during the dry season.

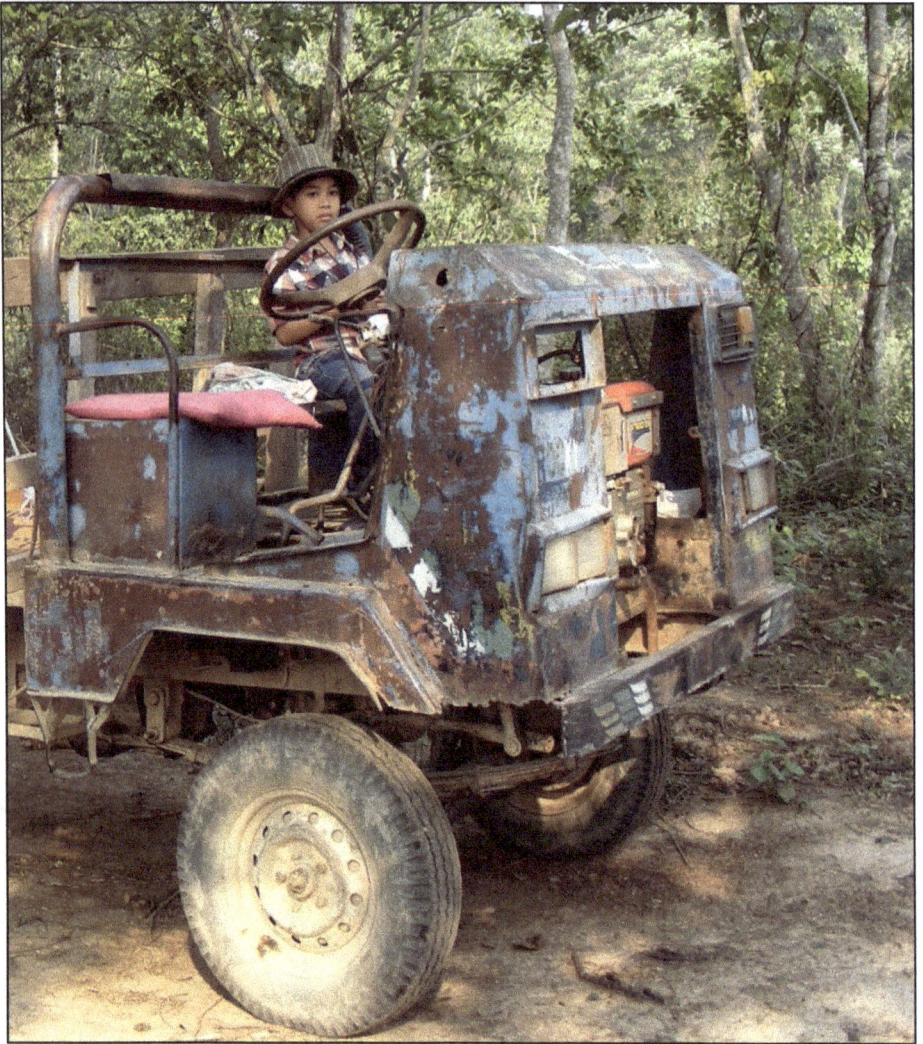

Mrs. Yod La's son, Sam, joined us on our visit to the forest as a passenger in the farm truck. Their family lives on the farm beside the Ing River along with 400 villagers. The Ing River is important spawning habitat for Mekong River fish, and parts of the river are a fish sanctuary that the locals call a "fish palace." The government has threatened to cut down the forest around the river and use the land for rice farming.

Map of the Mekong Ecosystems along Thai-Lao Border
Local Knowledge-based Research by Riverine Communities

In the afternoon, we come back to the Mekong School to visit and look at their maps and literature before we jump in the longboat to tour the Mekong River. The School undertakes research about the river and all of its aquatic life and ecology as well as the ways that local people use the river for their livelihood. The research collected by the School is used to inform decision-makers in the government about why the Mekong River should be protected and why the local tribal people should be able to stay on their land near the river.

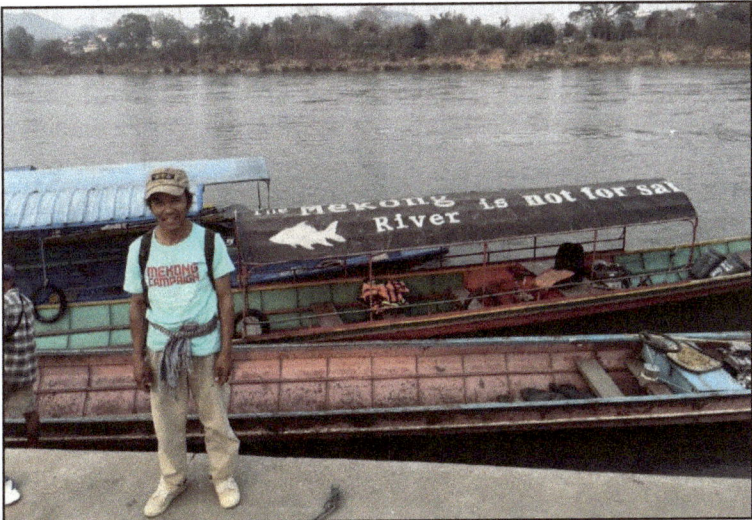

The School's 20-meter longboat boasts its credentials on the canopy – "The Mekong River Is Not For Sale!" Mr. Chak's hat echoes the same river-saving sentiment. The river is the center of the culture for tribal people as well as for the more modern culture that is encroaching on the Hill Tribe areas of Northern Thailand. Mr. Chak and his group believe that the Mekong River should be for nature and people, not "for sale" to the highest bidders in business.

The Mekong River is used for transportation – crops and food travel up and down the river by longboat. Some of these boats have large inboard motors that run on propane; others have outboard motor with spinning propellers at the end of 10-foot long shafts. The river bursts with the noise of boat traffic, fisherman, and even local students hollering out commands as they row crew. A small fish encampment on the Laos side of the river sits idle in the late afternoon as most of the

fishing is done in the morning along the Mekong River. The Mekong School for Local Knowledge focuses heavily on research about the fish, their habitat, and the ways of the fishermen along the river. By understanding the local knowledge, the School can influence decisions about the future of the river and help protect it from more dams.

For example, the School has researched 93 fish species in the Mekong River, 83 of which are native, 10 non-native. Thirteen of the Mekong's fish are officially "endangered" including the world famous "Giant Catfish" which can grow to over 200 kilograms. The operation of the Chinese dams upstream cause the river to be too cold, clear, and deep in the dry season because they run the water out through the hydroelectric turbines at a steady and unnatural rate in order to generate electricity. This, in turn, has led to the endangerment of some of the fish.

The Mekong River is under siege by more proposed dams. Large political disputes in all of the countries across the Mekong River's watershed underscore the significance of the river to this section of Southeast Asia. Governments have formed the "Mekong River Commission" to try and address the disputes. NGOs throughout the six-country region have alternatively formed the "Save The Mekong Coalition" to protect the river from dams. If all of the dams are built, the river will be devastated, along with the local people's livelihood and the fish, bird, and aquatic species that depend on the river for survival. (Image: ResearchGate.net)

In recent years, the Chinese government traveled by boat down to this section of the Mekong River near Chiang Khong in Thailand and attempted to blast the rocks out of the river to make it easier for ships to navigate its waters. The Mekong School for Local Knowledge has opposed the blasting – the rocks and rapids in the river are important bird-nesting and fish-spawning habitat.

"We are the children of the Mekong River," says Mr. Niwat Roykaew who is the Director of the Mekong School for Local Knowledge.

After our trip up the river, we visit with Mr. Niwat who is locally famous for boarding a Chinese ship that was attempting to blast the rocks out of the river a few years ago. Mr. Niwat kept the blasting at bay for several days until the Chinese government agreed to stop the work. Mr. Niwat speaks about the river in spiritual terms and sees the relationship between the river and the people as holistic. "When the river has problems, the people have problems," he says. "When the people re-learn their local knowledge and their relationship with the river, they can rebuild themselves as well as fight to protect the river."

"When I see the Mekong River, I see more than water. I see people, culture, fish, water, everything." – Mr. Niwat Roykaew

This is Mr. Niwat's desk – and also serves as the Mekong School's lunch table – on the banks of the river. Mr. Niwat sees the main threats to the river as dams, destruction of rocks and rapids, agricultural chemicals, garbage thrown into the river from ships, development in wetlands, and illegal fishing techniques like blasting and electro-shock.

"When local people learn their history, they are empowered by that knowledge," Mr. Niwat says. Researching all of the local history, relating that knowledge to decision-makers, and teaching that history to members of the Hill Tribes is the work of the Mekong School for Local Knowledge under Mr. Niwat's stewardship. Mr. Niwat has served as an expert witness in Thai court, arguing for better protection of the river and the landscapes and people who live around it. He is also frequently quoted in Southeast Asian newspapers as a key spokesperson for local and indigenous people fighting for their livelihoods along the river.

Chak Kineessee, left; Gary Wockner, right.

--end--

Will Oil Destroy This Mayan Village In Belize?

(*TckTckTck* and *Boulder Weekly*, February 2016)

Andres Coy is the "Alcalde," Mayan spiritual leader of Crique Sarco.

His face is lined, his skin the color the muddy Temash River we just crossed, and his hair jet black. When he says, "There's no money that can fix the river – you can't buy back the river," he says it with the authority he carries as the Mayan spiritual leader, the "Alcalde," in the village.

I believe him.

The river is full of sediment washed off from the surrounding rainforest, the wettest area in Belize. When we crossed the river into the village of Crique Sarco two hours ago, we entered Sarstoon Temash National Park, known locally as the "land between the rivers," an area that borders Guatemala. We are deep in Mayan country, and as our truck pulled into the village, our guide jumped out and walked across the lush grass to find the village leaders we've come to meet.

We got here after driving about an hour on a rough dirt road, the first forty-five minutes of which was in better shape because it had been rebuilt by an oil company. Oil has come to the Mayans, and we are here for oil too – to learn how this small and very rural Mayan village is protecting its people and native lands from the threat of oil.

The leaders of this Mayan community have agreed to meet me so I can help tell their story about their fight with oil. I'm here with a NGO called "SATIIM" which stands for "Sarstoon-Temash Institute For Indigenous Management." The Temash River and Sarstoon River border the Park, the land in between is about 42,000 acres, and indigenous Mayan country covers the Park and everything around us for miles in every direction. SATIIM's mission is to promote and protect the rights of these indigenous people and to safeguard the ecological integrity of the region. That's a very difficult and serious business with one oil well already drilled by an American company and others pending.

Villagers live on common ground in wood houses with thatch roofs.

We take a short tour of the village which has about sixty families. It's Sunday, just before lunchtime, and the village is very quiet – some of the villagers are still in "Sunday Prayer" inside their homes. The homes are mixed frame with thatched roofs. There's running water in a few homes, but not in most. The village is clean – in fact it's cleaner than most of the Belizean towns I'd spent the last 10 days visiting in other parts of the country. Chickens strut around free-ranging and a couple of friendly dogs follow us along as we visit a very small store and then use a shared outhouse.

After the brief tour, we sit down in a small thatched-roof home around a plastic folding table. There's a few electric generators in the village, but they're not running, and so there's no lights in the hut. My eyes adjust to the darkness after a few minutes.

SATIIM's Executive Director, Froyla Tzalam, set up this meeting and brought me here, and is sitting across the table. Froyla and I got acquainted over dinner last night in Punta Gorda, the nearest small city (5,000 people) which is the hub of Southern Belize and where the office of SATIIM is located. Small Mayan villages – some of which are very rural like this one – are dotted along the roads stretching miles away from Punta Gorda. Froyla is a fireball – outspoken, whip smart, and filled with energy. She is also a Mayan and entrusted by the various communities that make up SATIIM to represent their voices which is often

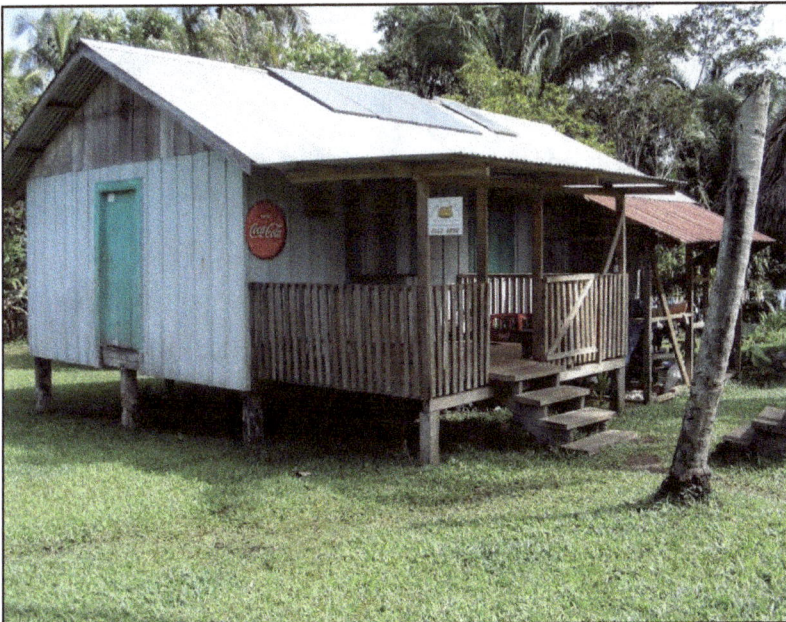

One of the village stores has solar panels.

against the Belizean government as well as the American oil company. They have picked their leader well.

The five Mayan community leaders, all men, slowly walk in and sit around the room, while two Mayan women bring in food. Rice and beans, chicken, a pork stew, and a spicy soup are the menu. All are delicious as we make small talk through lunch. Almost everyone in Belize is bilingual, and the Mayans all know English as a second language – it is taught in the village school – and so we can understand each other very well though they apologize for their English unnecessarily. As we finish, the food and dishes are whisked away and the table wiped clean. There's a long and pregnant pause before Froyla speaks and brings us to the reason for the meeting, for me to hear their stories and learn about their concerns for the oil drilling in their homelands.

Marcos Chub, who is the Mayor of the community speaks first, and slowly, but then warms up as the words flow troublingly from his mouth. He speaks for a few minutes and immediately notes that this is a difficult fight – the village is fighting both the government and the oil company over rights to their land and for protection of their environment. "They put everything sweet, like candy," he says, referring to how the oil company and the Belizean government have tried to sell oil drilling to the local Mayans. "But the decision should be made by our community, not the government. It brings concerns because of the environmental threats. It could damage our river – our villages fish downstream and hunt as well."

Everyone watches and listens to Marcos and no one interrupts him, and when he finishes, there's another long pause. Andres Coy, the village's Mayan spiritual leader and Alcalde, speaks next and more directly.

"The voice of the village must be heard," he says. "The government doesn't respect our community. The government doesn't care about the people, they just care about the money. Pollution is going to be in the air we breathe, the animals and fishes we eat. Yes, there will be jobs, but there will be a price to the environment."

Andres talks about the river as I noted above, and adds, "We believe we are the owners of the resources and the courts have formally recognized that." Andres is matter of fact in his statement, and for good reason. On behalf of the Mayan communities, SATIIM sued the federal government and won, and when the government appealed the suit twice, SATIIM won both times including with the highest court at the Caribbean Court of Justice. Just weeks before my arrival, the Caribbean Court ruled and has now forced the government to establish some type of land rights for the Mayan people in the region.

Marcos speaks again and is now more excited as the energy in the room grows.

"The government has a tricky idea and hired public relations people to give us false information," he said.

Andres backs this up by saying, "They think the indigenous people don't have common sense to know what's good for us."

The Temash River is full of sediment after a morning rainstorm.

As the discussion develops, it becomes very clear that SATIIM has played a critical role in educating and informing the local village, which has intermittent electricity and internet access. Among other things, SATIIM has visited with the community many times, provided technical information, including a professional review of the "environmental impact assessment" for the oil drilling, and provides weekly radio broadcasts that are heard throughout the region

At one point, Andres says, "Thank god SATIIM is helping us."

The conversation continues for another hour as each leader speaks. They support each other with snippets of their own, the overall story becoming clearer. The men tell stories of how the oil company ran survey lines across their land, and didn't ask for permission as the company cut new roads right through some of their farms. The men don't believe anything the oil company says. The men say the government wants money and is trying to force oil exploration and production down their throats. Several of the men say the government and the oil company are providing "false information" to the communities.

The men tell me that the Mayan people want control of their land and the resources underneath it. The Mayans are not necessarily saying "no" to oil drilling, but they want to be consulted in the decision, and if oil drilling happens, they want part of the money. The number "five percent" has been mentioned a couple times – prior to the court rulings, if oil was produced on their lands, the Mayans would have gotten nothing. If nothing else, they want five percent of price of the oil produced on their lands. They are wrestling with this conundrum of pollution and money and oil, their faces furrowed and their voices aching from the wrestling match. "We are thinking for future generations. The ground is like our mother; she feeds us," says Andres.

The village school was recently painted, including with the logo of the oil company.

After everyone has had a turn at speaking, I feel compelled to speak myself. I had been holding my tongue as I heard the stories. I also begin slowly but quickly get to the point.

"I'm from the state of Colorado in the United States," I say. "Within 100 miles of my house, there are over 22,000 active oil and gas wells." When I say this, everyone in the room gasps. Their attention is now riveted. So far they have had one single well drilled four miles away, and it has created an enormous conflict and uproar.

I continue, "The air pollution is sometimes worse than downtown Los Angeles. The groundwater has been polluted, and oil has been spilled into our rivers. The landscape has been decimated, criss-crossed and carved into little pieces."

I pause and say, "I urge you to be very careful and very vigilant. Once you allow the drilling, you can never go back."

"Be very vigilant," I repeat, slowly. Everyone nods

After a few more questions and comments, our conversation ends and we step outside. The mood brightens as the humid sunshine pours through the village canopy. We take a few photos and say good-byes. As Froyla, our guide, and I head back to our truck, we walk by the village school which was recently repainted by the oil company, U.S. Capital Energy, which emblazoned their name and logo on the school in exchange for the paint job. When I ask about the name and paint, our guide says, "camouflage" – more candy from the oil company.

We get in the truck and drive back across the Temash River, leaving their village and heading back on the rough dirt road. After about 15 minutes, we reach the turnoff that leads down to where the oil company drilled the well. The road is gated with a "no trespassing sign" and a young man sits in civilian clothes in the guard house. When he sees us, he moves behind a wall out of sight.

Like oil drilling everywhere on the planet, the price has plunged here in Belize and the oil company has stopped exploring and drilling, for now. U.S. Capital Energy is a privately held company and information sharing is sparse. From the villagers' stories, it's unclear if and how much oil and was found, and at what depth, and at what price point it is recoverable. Belize has many active oil wells, and drilling and production are occurring across the nearby border in Guatemala. It's likely that oil will come to this village eventually.

As the roads smooths out – now rebuilt with oil money – and we make our way another 45 minutes back to the paved road, I consider what I really wanted to tell the Mayans. I was there as a guest to hear and tell their stories, not to tell them what I thought they should do. But what I wanted to say was that if oil

Gary Wockner, left, with the village leaders and Froyla Tzalam.

comes here, this place will never be the same. Roads will crisscross your village lands, the river will be polluted, wildlife will leave, the air will be brown and stink, the landscape will become an industrialized nightmare completely different than this quiet village you live in now. You will be left with nothing.

And if you do negotiate a five percent royalty, your lives will be forever changed. I did the math quickly in my head as I sat in the hut. At $20 million per well over 20 years, and with just 20 wells in the entire area of the village's farmland and rainforest, you're looking at roughly $50,000 per person per year, which is likely 10 times more than any of them make as farmers. This serene, indigenous little village would bust apart – culturally, financially, psychologically – and never be the same.

When we hit the paved road, we turn south and can see the lush jungle of the Mayan Hills in the background. Froyla's eyes light up and she says, "I just love this view. The Mayan Hills are so beautiful."

For now, I think to myself.

--end--

Will Climate Change Swamp Cartagena?

(*Waterkeeper*, January 2016)

It's November 2015 and I'm walking along the streets of Old Town Cartagena, Columbia, just a couple blocks from the Caribbean Sea. It's supposed to be the rainy season here where it rains almost every day, but it hasn't rained for two months. Still, there's a small amount of water running in the gutters in many of these Cartagena streets. I keep looking around to see where the water is coming from – people washing cars? Vendors washing off vegetables? Where is it coming from? It's in almost every gutter on every street.

Elizabeth Ramirez is the Cartagena Baykeeper

"Climate change," says my colleague and guide for two days, Elizabeth Ramirez, who is a professor of environmental law and the Cartagena Baykeeper representing the International Waterkeeper Alliance in this port city.

"What?" I respond.

Elizabeth speaks in broken English, and I respond to her in even worse Spanish, but she finally explains, "Sea level rise. It doesn't rain anymore, but the sea is rising up in the ground."

When you think about sea level rise, you think about the sea rising up and coming over the beaches and rocks in storm surges, but here in Cartagena the rising sea has also increased the height of the groundwater under the city and the water is coming up through the gutters in the streets. This fact provides a cruel irony in Old Town Cartagena – the area is surrounded by a nearly 400 year-old 15-foot high stone wall which is an immense fortress designed to keep out invading armies. Now, the threat comes from underneath the city, an invader the Spanish colonials could have never imagined and from which the wall may do little to protect the city.

Sea levels have been rising in the Caribbean and Cartagena at a rate of about 1 inch per 10 years. Storm surges have occasionally already swamped small sections of the city that are very near sea level. Of further concern, scientists predict that sea level rise will be worse in the equatorial region of the planet, putting much of the Caribbean at risk including Cartagena and all around the Gulf of Mexico.

The City of Cartagena has been grappling with the sea level rise problem for at least a decade. In the glitzy touristy section of town – which is called Boca Grande, just south of Old Town – the City is building a 3-foot high retaining wall to keep out the rising sea and Cartagena Bay. As Elizabeth and I drive around

Elizabeth Ramriz stands in front of the small sea wall that is supposed to protect Cartagena's tourist district from climate change-caused sea level rise.

the tourist area, we stop to look at the retaining wall under construction – it seems too small to me, more like "underfunded hope" rather than a large-scale public-works project that this and other Caribbean cities will need to actually protect themselves from climate change. Again though, there's a concern that the wall will only address part of the problem related to storm surges because the increasing groundwater levels are also making the streets and gutters wet in Boca Grande. As we drive around the hotels, water splashed under our tires though a drop of rain had not fallen in weeks.

Cartagena Bay is large, nearly 40 square miles, and as we motor-boat around it the next day, the immensity of the bay and the environmental problems flowing into and around it feel genuinely overwhelming. Cartagena is a growing and bustling Latin American port city with myriad pollution problems – pollution from the tourist industry, the large industrial port, and the growing population (much of which lives in extreme poverty) – in addition to the major issue of climate change. These problems are clearly visible in Cartagena Bay which used

Local fisherman in a dugout canoe with makeshift paddles fish amidst the massive container ports and oil tankers in Cartagena Bay.

to be clear but is now a kind of murky green-brown color with visibility of only a foot or two.

Over the last few decades, a bustling international tourist economy has developed along the Caribbean coast in Cartagena. Dozens of high-rise hotels, international flights, and some glitzy restaurants cater to the tourist industry. Along with the tourists also comes pollution, most of it as water pollution from the hotels and their wastewater treatment facilities that fail to keep up with the growth. Like many growing Latin American cities, Cartagena has fairly good environmental laws, but monitoring and enforcement of polluters is lagging and corruption is common. Over 15 years ago the World Bank targeted Cartagena with a grant to address the sewage problem, and the City of Cartagena continues to grapple with the growth in the tourist industry, but sewage problems persist in the bay, in the nearby Cienega de la Virgin, and in the Caribbean Sea along the beach.

The large and growing industrial port is also a significant polluter of Cartagena Bay. Oil, gas, bananas, and coffee beans (remember Juan Valdez?) are the

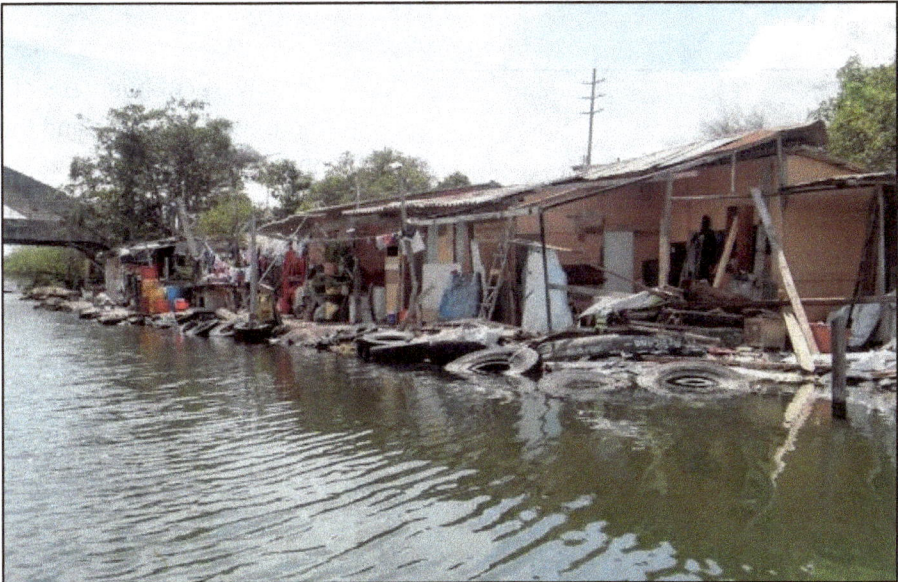

Extreme poverty surrounds much of Cartagena Bay -- people live in makeshift shacks along the polluted water.

largest exported products. Enormous chemical plants, fossil fuel powerplants, and container-ship terminals line much of the bay. The City of Cartagena and

Columbian authorities struggle to regulate these polluters, some of which are immensely wealthy and powerful, including ExxonMobil. All along the bay as we boat along – and as we drove through the industrial section the day before – I see numerous ditches leading into the bay which are filled with garbage and muck often running within feet of massive oil tanks, chemical facilities, and other industrial carnage.

Amidst the bustling tourist and industrial activity lives a vast swath of people in extreme poverty, many living at subsistence level and feeding off of the fish in Cartagena Bay. A 2009 NPR report identified massive wealth disparities in the city, "misery malnourishment and disease," and "raw sewage flowing down unpaved streets." Another 2009 report in the Seattle Times, called it "Cartagena's Hidden Shame," where over 600,000 of the 1 million people in the city live in poverty, many in complete slums. As I traveled throughout the city and as we motor along the bay, I am struck by the poverty – mass numbers of people living in tin shacks, under bridges, or completely homeless. Garbage is absolutely everywhere – plastic bags and plastic bottles make up the most of it – and when it rains in Cartagena the garbage flowing into the bay makes it inhospitable.

Gary Wockner (r), Elizabeth Ramirez, and a colleague from a local university.

The poverty of hundreds of thousands of people and the pollution is stunning. The juxtaposition of a wealthy tourist business and industrial port against this poverty is apparent everywhere. Subsistence fishermen paddle dilapidated canoes with makeshift paddles right in front of a huge multi-national corporate container port. Massive oil tankers motor through the bay making waves that slap up against tin shacks filled with children and families. Right across the bay from glitzy tourist hotels are thousands of shanties and slums, garbage hanging in the mangroves, and people living and feeding from the bay's water which is filled with pollution.

Elizabeth Ramirez – the Cartagena Baykeeper – is a small, solid woman. She's serious, and she needs to be. If you think the odds against you are a million to one, you might know how she feels. There's not much support for environmentalists in Columbia or in Cartagena, the problems are immense and growing, and like environmental advocates everywhere she is understaffed and overburdened. But with the odds against her, she is steadfastly marshalling a team of colleagues to help move her mission of protecting the bay forward.

Elizabeth teaches and does research at three different universities in Cartagena, all three of which we visited to meet with her colleagues. With a law degree, a doctorate, and other specialist degrees hanging on her wall in her home-office of the Cartagena Baykeeper, Elizabeth is working to put together a coalition of scientists, policymakers, and students to create a campaign that monitors for

Map of the Cartagena area.

pollution, enforces the environmental laws of Columbia, and organizes the local community to celebrate their watery heritage that surrounds Cartagena.

Specifically in 2016, Elizabeth is putting together a week-long series of events that will bring together Waterkeeper activists from around Latin America, focus a few days on the climate change problem, and then finish up with a multi-day "Cultural Festival of Water" along the bay and the Cienega to help galvanize the local community – rich and poor alike – to appreciate and protect Cartagena's water. She's even reached out to oil and chemical companies and is optimistic they will engage with the effort, for they too are vulnerable to climate change as their ports are threatened by the rising sea levels.

After our boat trip around Cartagena Bay, Elizabeth and her nephew drive me back to my hotel in Boca Grande. We communicate poorly due to our language difficulties, but I feel that I understand exactly what she has been telling me the last two days. "To protect the bay and the Cienega, the people will need to be organized to help them celebrate their water culture," she says to me. Elizabeth knows well that the problems of environmental degradation and social justice are completely intertwined in Cartagena, and that the solution must engage with the culture of people.

At less than five feet tall, Elizabeth Ramirez is barely taller than the cement wall the City is building to protect Cartagena Bay from climate change. She too seems like "underfunded hope" rather than the large-scale project needed to address the local environmental problems. But Elizabeth is driven – driven to protect the bay and organize her community to celebrate the watery world surrounding it.

--end--

Europe's Dirty Little Secret: Moroccan Slaves and a 'Sea of Plastic'

(EcoWatch, December 2015)

It seemed like a wonderful idea—driving the Spanish coast from Barcelona all the way down to the Straits of Gibraltar. We got there in April, right before tourist season, and happily missed much of the vacationing European onslaught. Our goal was to hit the smaller less-touristy beach towns to do some diving, paddleboarding and beachcombing along the Mediterranean Coast.

South of Barcelona, we stayed in L'Ampolla and enjoyed near-deserted beaches, hotels and restaurants. Next stop was Altea—absolutely beautiful, also with few tourists, and with that amazing wall of mountains as the backdrop, the Sierra de Bernia. Further along the coast, the water was the most curious blue I'd seen in El Portus, and had the wind and surf not been pounding, it would have been a great place to paddleboard and sea kayak.

Standup paddleboarding near the waterfall of Nerja, Spain. Photo: PaddleInSpain.com

But it was just south of El Portus, after the city of Mazarron along E-15 where we started seeing the first few greenhouses.

I was there with Catherine Ebeling—bestselling author of diet and health books—and I am an environmental activist, and so for the two of us, the idea of greenhouses seemed quaint and healthy, at first. It was like: "Look at that, greenhouses, what a great way to create sustainability and locally grown food." But as we motored along E-15—through the desert valley and then finally into the cities in and around Campo Hermoso—the landscape changed dramatically. It went from a view of the beautiful azure Mediterranean Sea with gently sloping hills and mountains, to patches of white plastic here and there, expanding to greater and greater expanses of white plastic, until it became almost solid white plastic covering the landscape as far as the eye could see, blotting out everything.

They call it a "Sea of Plastic" and the "vast expanse of polytunnels." The further we drove, nearer and through Almeria into the city of El Ejido, I started thinking of it as the apocalypse. But the visual onslaught is the least of the problem—news articles have reported on the issues with the greenhouses many times, environmental groups have tried to address the problem and governments have launched efforts to mitigate it.

Greenhouses cover every square inch of land, more than 165 square miles of land around Almeria, Spain.

As we drove along, the smell of plastic and chemicals permeated the car and offered the first scent of the larger environmental problem. The greenhouses are almost all hydroponic—growing vegetables in water, air and a chemical stew of fertilizer, herbicide and pesticide. Due to the hot and extremely difficult working conditions inside the greenhouses, almost all of the human labor is imported, much of it slave-like from Africa.

The growth in greenhouses started in the late 1970s as a local response to an economic opportunity to provide vegetables to the European marketplace. The transformed landscape has also transformed the economy from a land of farmers struggling in dry rocky soil in the 1970s to an economy of extremely wealthy greenhouse owners. By 2004, thousands of small landowners had turned their entire property—every square inch—into greenhouse farms as the vegetables started appearing in grocery stores and restaurants across the European continent, especially in the UK and also in Paris. In the 2000s, immigrants from Africa—many with no legal papers—were shipped in by the hundreds per boatload to work in the plastic greenhouses.

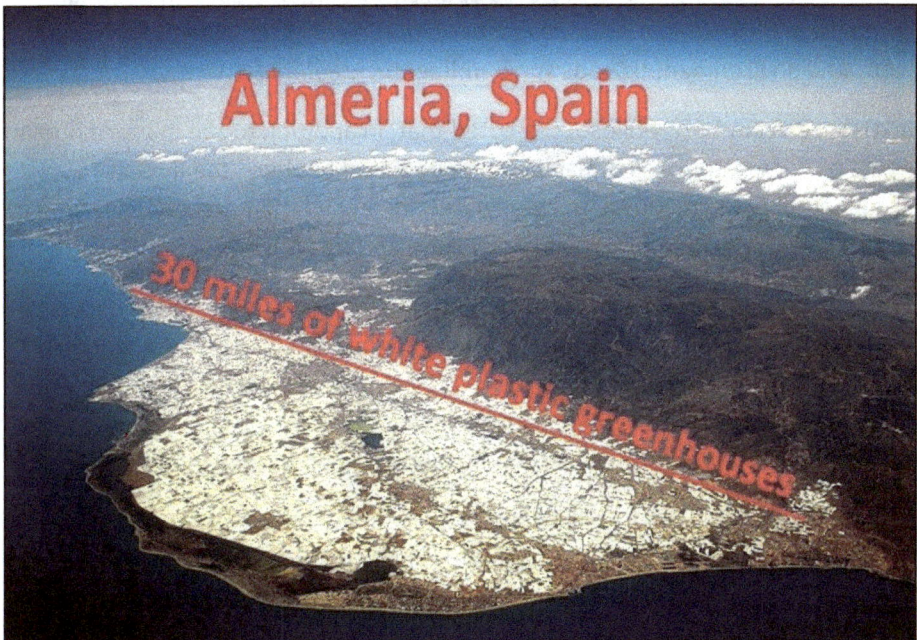

They call it a "Sea of Plastic" and a "Vast Expanse of Polytunnels."

By 2011, a news report in The Guardian said that more than 100,000 workers toil away inside the greenhouses, many living in "inhuman" slums and laboring in the chemical stew. The report noted:

- "Migrant workers from Africa living in shacks made of old boxes and plastic sheeting, without sanitation or access to drinking water.

- Wages that are routinely less than half the legal minimum wage.

- Workers without papers being told they will be reported to the police if they complain.

- Allegations of segregation enforced by police harassment when African workers stray outside the hothouse areas into tourist areas."

A 2013 documentary film, *The Morrocan Slaves of El Ejido, Spain (Esclave marocain a El Ejido, Espagne)*, chronicled the plight of the migrant workers toiling inside the hot greenhouses as well as their difficult lives outside of work.

In 2014, amidst a large controversy, a Spanish TV station created a fictional crime drama, *Plastic Sea (Mar de Plastico),* that highlighted much of the crime, labor and environmental chaos surrounding the greenhouse farms.

A 2015 report in NaturPhilosophie noted that, in addition to the massive human rights problems, the area is plagued with depleted aquifers, the largest desalination plant in Europe to keep water flowing into the greenhouses, and rising cancer rates due to pesticide exposure among workers.

Waste from the "farms" is reported to run off into the Mediterranean Sea, including the chemical waste, plastic waste and human waste of the workers. Entire industries have popped up in the area simply to make the massive amount of plastic for the greenhouses which has a short lifespan and is sometimes discarded, strewn across the landscape or washed into the sea.

Some observers call it a $1 billion "miracle economy," while others call it the "exploitation of cheap labor with no rights" and "environmental devastation." The swath of greenhouses is massive enough to be seen from space and has been described as a "Dystopian Sea."

The area is so large that it actually creates its own "albedo effect" because it reflects the sun's rays and cools the atmosphere. Scientists claim that local temperatures have actually decreased by 1 degree since 1980, while other areas of Spain have increased by 1 to 3 degrees over the same time period.

All of the negative publicity has caused the greenhouse corporations, as well as the local governments, to combat the tide of news stories with greenwashed news releases that, among other things, even brag about the albedo effect by saying that the greenhouses serve a public good by cooling the climate on the Southern Iberian Peninsula. The controversy continues to escalate month-by-month as the number of greenhouses increase and stretch farther and farther up and down the coastline.

Image of greenhouses of Almeria, Spain from space. Photo credit: NASA

As we drove through and beyond El Ejido, the greenhouses continued to stretch along the road in La Rabita and Carchuna. Finally, in the tourist area of Nerja, we could see no more greenhouses—from the road at least—and a sense of relief set in. The drive was very unsettling, causing a tightness in our chests and cringe on our faces—the continual glare of the white and the smell of plastic and chemicals gave us headaches that we tried to wash away with long gulps of bottled water.

As we dined that evening in Nerja, we ordered a salad the same as we had in restaurants all across southern Europe. The romaine lettuce, bell peppers, tomatoes, cucumbers and carrots took on an all new look and flavor now colored by our education about the source of the food. The waitress proudly exclaimed that the salad was "locally grown."

The next morning we rented standup paddleboards and paddled along the cliffs just north of Nerja. The Mediterranean Sea was quiet and crystalline clear. A few hundred yards north of Nerja we paddled under a beautiful waterfall careening over the cliff above and splashing into the Sea. The fresh water felt wonderful washing over my head, clearing the dystopian sea of plastic from my brain.

But then we paddled a few hundred yards farther south and saw greenhouses perched on the cliffs above and stretching intermittently along the coast. It seemed like the greenhouses were everywhere. When I got back to our hotel that night I looked on Google Earth, and indeed, the stream from the waterfall ran right through acres of greenhouses up on the cliffs that we couldn't see from the water below. Was that lovely waterfall actually a toxic stream of runoff from the plastic greenhouses?

NaturPhilosophie reports that tens of millions of acres of land across the planet are now covered by plastic greenhouses or plastic mulch directly on top of ground. Eighty five percent of those greenhouses are in Asia. The future presented by the greenhouses of Almeria, Spain, is not a clean eco-tech environment like in the Biosphere project in the desert of Arizona that Americans are familiar with. Conversely, it's an environmental dystopia filled with slave-like labor, chemical-laden food and intense heat. Is this the new wave of farming? An apocalyptic world covered by plastic may await us.

--end--

Dams Cause Climate Change, They Are Not Clean Energy

(*EcoWatch*, August 2014)

People believe hydroelectric dams provide clean energy. It's not true.

I don't blame the public or the media for making this false claim—I've heard it come out of the mouth of the biggest dam operator in the Southwest U.S., and the media often repeats it. Unfortunately, it was further repeated in a horribly misguided "study" put out by the U.S. Dept of Energy in April 2015.

Glen Canyon Dam, Arizona.

But when I heard it quoted three months ago in a May 12 *New Yorker* story out of the mouth of Mark Tercek who is CEO of The Nature Conservancy to rationalize his organization's support of new dams in Columbia, I knew it's time to once-again address this disastrous myth.

Tercek is quoted as saying: "Environmentalists generally hate dams, even though they're clean energy."

Dams are not "clean energy." Dams are, in fact, causing climate change. A growing body of science is studying just how bad dams are. Here are the issues:

• Organic material—vegetation, sediment and soil—flows from rivers into reservoirs and decomposes emitting methane and carbon dioxide into the water and then the air throughout the hydro-electric generation cycle. Studies indicate that where organic material is the highest (in the tropics or in high sediment areas) hydro-electric dams can actually emit more greenhouse gases than coal-fired powerplants. These methane emissions are not limited to tropical areas; they occur in the U.S. too. "Methane springs" are widely reported on the mud flats of Lake Powell which is a reservoir behind Glen Canyon Dam on the Colorado River, and "trains" of "methane bubbles" have been reported floating on Lake Powell. As far back as 1948, the U.S. Geological Survey examined what they then called "gas pits" in the mud flats of Lake Mead which is a reservoir behind Hoover Dam on the Colorado River. As a real conversation ender, Brazil's National Institute of Space Research estimates that "dams are the largest single [human-caused] source of methane, being responsible for 23 percent of all methane emissions due to human activities."

• Large dams contain enormous amounts of cement which during the construction process uses massive amounts of energy that emits greenhouse gas emissions. For one medium-sized dam project proposed for the Cache la Poudre River in Colorado, it is estimated that the construction would emit 218,000 metric tons CO2-equivalents which equals the emissions from almost 46,000 automobiles on the road for one year. Larger dams, such as Hoover Dam which contains 4.36 million cubic yards of concrete, would have exponentially higher climate change impacts from construction. The largest hydro-electric dam on the planet—the Three Gorges Dam in China—contains 27.15 million cubic meters of cement.

• Dams that divert water out of rivers may have significant additional climate change impacts because they drain and dry up downstream wetlands that are "carbon sinks" holding vast amounts of greenhouse gases in soils. This draining and dry-up causes carbon and methane to be released and emitted into the air. A proposal for a dam on the Cache la Poudre River in Colorado would dry up 1,700 acres of wetlands thus emitting about 7,000 metric tons of CO2 equivalents. As just one more example, when the Colorado River was diverted and drained, the dams and diversions dried up about 2 million acres of wetlands in the former Colorado River Delta—the climate change impact of destroying those wetlands was likely staggering.

- Some dams, like the proposed massive ecosystem-wide Belo Monte dams on the Amazon River in Brazil, also include massive deforestation plans on areas that will be flooded by behind the reservoirs. The deforestation itself would release enormous amounts of greenhouse gas emissions.

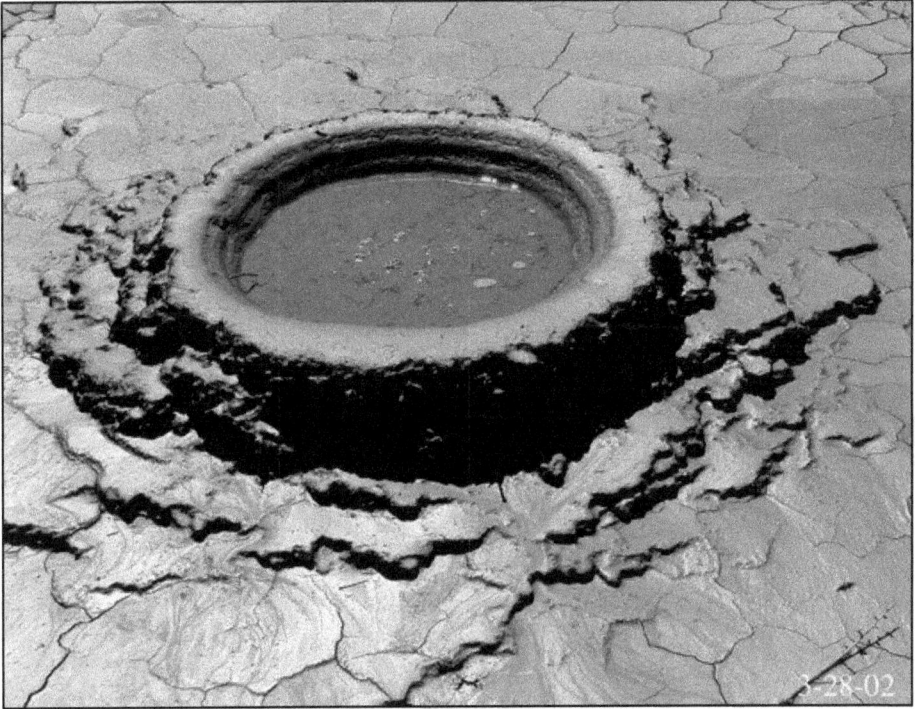

"Methane springs" are widely reported on the mud flats of Lake Powell which is a reservoir behind Glen Canyon Dam on the Colorado River and "trains" of "methane bubbles" have been reported floating on Lake Powell.

Just how much of climate change is caused by dams and reservoirs is not completely known—we need more research before we build any more dams and potentially make a terrible mistake based on myths, propaganda and false information.

Some hydro-electric dams and reservoirs are not as bad as others—some may be worse climate change emitters than coal power plants, most are likely better. But, most hydro-electric dams are likely much worse climate change emitters than wind or solar power, so saying that hydro-electric is better than coal power is just a straw-man argument unsupported by the science and economics of 21st century renewable energy. Increasingly, wind and solar is cheaper, faster and cleaner.

Further, many dams and reservoirs are not hydro-electric plants at all and are only used for water storage and diversion, in which case they absolutely increase climate change emissions when they're built and every single day they continue to exist.

Dams are not clean energy and everyone involved with dams and energy— hydro-plant operators, media, government officials and environmentalists— must stop saying it.

Dams cause climate change. Period.

--end--

The Hydropower Methane Bomb No One Wants to Talk About

(*EcoWatch* and *Waterkeeper Magazine* October 2015)

As we stood on our boards and paddled away from the cove at Malpais and turned south past the wave-break, I felt a rush of what Costa Ricans call *pura vida*—"pure life." The wind was calm, the sun glaring, and the sea slightly rolling along this headland that includes the 3,000-acre Cabo Blanco National Park. Our guide, Andy Seidensticker, had moved to Costa Rica just to surf and paddleboard these waves at the southern tip of the Nicoya Peninsula on the Pacific coast.

Pura Vida in Costa Rica?

There are blessings as well as problems amid Costa Rica's abundant waters. Poudre Riverkeeper Gary Wockner felt the rush of what locals call "pure life" on a paddleboarding trip off the Nicoya Peninsula near Malpais.

This excursion with Carolina Chavarria, executive director of Nicoya Peninsula Waterkeeper, topped off my water-filled trip to Costa Rica this past winter. With the park to our left, we paddled just outside the wave-break, chatting, watching wildlife, soaking in the sun until we reached a warm freshwater spring that bubbled up in the ocean about 100 meters offshore. Surrounded by the bubbles, we sat on our boards and rested before paddling back to the cove. As the wind picked up and swells rose higher, the return paddling became more strenuous, as did our conversation about the watery challenges facing Costa Rica.

There are as many problems as blessings in the country's abundant waters, and Chavarria and her staff are energetically confronting those problems, many of which are caused by the country's booming tourist industry. Costa Rica has exemplary environmental laws but they are poorly enforced. Restaurants, hotels, and home- and road-construction generate sewage and runoff that flow directly into rivers and the ocean.

In Santa Theresa, the home of the Nicoya Peninsula Waterkeeper, five miles from Malpais, the water supply descends from the country's inland mountains out of a massive and rapidly expanding network of dams and through a snaking tangle of canals, pipes and dikes. Many of Costa Rica's dams also produce hydroelectric power, which provides 80 percent of Costa Rica's electricity. Government and business officials speak of this as "clean energy" that is "carbon free." Nothing could be further from the truth.

A few months before visiting Costa Rica I had written a post for *EcoWatch*, "Dams Cause Climate Change: They Are Not Clean Energy." Based on research I'd done in fighting dam proposals on my own river, the Cache le Poudre, as well as my work advocating for the already-dammed Colorado River, I've come to believe that hydropower is one of the biggest environmental problems our planet faces. Construction of hydroelectric dams around the world is surging dramatically, guided by the false premise that they produce clean energy, even as study after study refutes this claim.

How Does Hydropower Cause Methane Emissions?

The principal environmental menace of hydroelectric dams is caused by organic material—vegetation, sediment and soil—that flows from rivers into reservoirs and decomposes, emitting methane and carbon dioxide into the water and the air throughout the generation cycle. Studies indicate that in tropical environments and high-sediment areas, where organic material is highest, dams can release more greenhouse gas than coal-fired power plants. Philip Fearnside, a research professor at the National Institute for Research in the Amazon, in Manaus, Brazil, and one of the most cited scientists on the subject of climate change, has called these dams "methane factories." And, according to Brazil's National Institute of Space Research, dams are "the largest single anthropogenic source of methane, being responsible for 23 percent of all methane emissions due to human activities."

"Hydropower is dirty energy, and should be treated just like fossil fuel."

Even that number 23 may be low; the emissions can be huge even in temperate climates. A 2014 article in Climate Central offered a disturbing comparison: "Imagine nearly 6,000 dairy cows doing what cows do, belching and being flatulent for a full year. That's how much methane was emitted from one Ohio reservoir in 2012. [Yet] reservoirs and hydropower are often thought of as climate-friendly because they don't burn fossil fuels to produce electricity." Another 2014 article in the same publication pointed out that, because very few dams and reservoirs are being studied, their methane emissions are mostly unaccounted for in climate-change analyses across the planet.

An article published in the 2013 book *Climate Governance in the Developing World* focused this failing on Costa Rica:

"These [methane] emissions, however, are neither measured nor taken into account in calculating Costa Rica's carbon balance. Given that the nation's electricity demand is projected to increase by 6 percent per year for the foreseeable future, and that the majority of this is to be met with increased hydroelectricity production, including such emissions in neutrality calculations would probably make it quite difficult for the country ever to achieve its goals."

Indeed, in February and March of this year, Costa Rica's government-owned electric utility issued press releases announcing that the country is on track to reach its "carbon neutrality" goals by 2021, stating that "88 percent of its electricity came from clean sources" in 2014 and that, during the first 75 days of 2015, it had been 100 percent powered by "clean" and "renewable" energy. News agencies across the world spread this misinformation about hydroelectric power. CNN claimed the prize for irresponsible reporting when it ran a TV news-segment, "A Carbonless Year for Costa Rica." More surprising still, some American environmentalists also took the bait. Green groups, including many national organizations, splashed the stories and scientifically false information across social media—350.org ran a large Facebook meme celebrating Costa Rica's achievement.

Hydropower's Methane Bomb Threatens COP 21

Even worse, the myth of carbon-free hydropower is embedded in the Kyoto protocol's "Clean Development Mechanism" to address planetary climate change, and is increasingly being implemented by countries in attendance at COP 21 in Paris. The program calls for a bigger investment in hydropower than in any other type of purported "clean energy." Such recommendations heavily influence funding-decisions made by the U.S. government and international lenders such as the World Bank and International Monetary Fund. In fact, the World Bank states on its website: "As demand grows for clean, reliable, affordable energy, along with the urgency of expanding access to reach the unserved, hydropower has assumed critical importance."

In the U.S. the Department of Energy published a report in 2014 calling for "new hydropower development across more than three million U.S. rivers and streams," and it is not unreasonable to fear that the United Nations Conference on Climate Change later this year in Paris will be polluted with "hydropower = clean energy" propaganda.

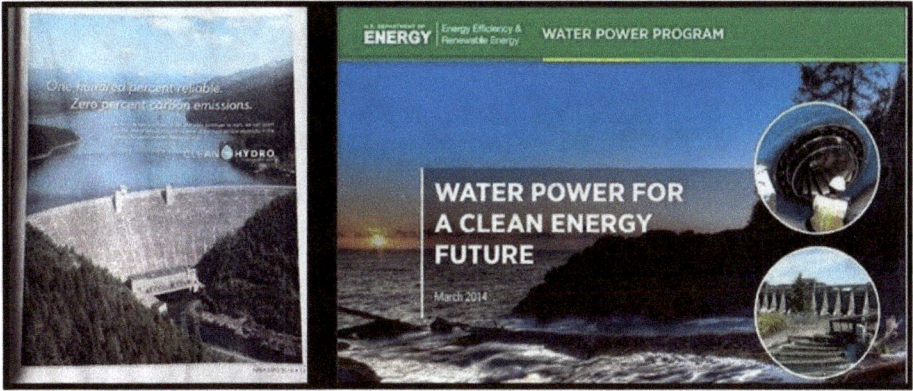

A U.S. government pamphlet touts the benefits of hydropower. Because very few of the world's dams are being studied, the huge amounts of methane they emit are mostly unaccounted for in climate-change analyses.

As governments and funders have gravitated more and more to hydropower over the last 10 years, the dam industry has accordingly ramped up its "green washing." It pretends, as it has for decades, that its activities are benign, while dams and reservoirs have flooded and displaced communities, destroyed rivers and perpetrated massive human rights abuses across the planet, under the false promise of "clean and renewable energy."

In the U.S., along the Colorado River, the directors of Glen Canyon and Hoover Dams, two of the biggest river-destruction schemes in human history, continue to claim those dams supply "clean energy" and erroneously calculate the "carbon offset" of their hydropower versus the alternative of coal power. In 2013, at a public meeting of 1,200 people in Las Vegas, I heard government officials make such claim, which have repeatedly been repudiated by Colorado Riverkeeper John Weisheit and others.

Like the tobacco industry refusing for decades to accept that its product causes cancer, the dam industry, in public statements and advertisements, flouts the science that links methane emissions to hydropower. And to make matters worse, the U.S. Department of Energy reinforces the myth of clean hydropower.

"Like the tobacco industry refusing for decades to accept that its product causes cancer, the dam industry flouts the science that links methane emissions to hydropower."

This myth seems to permeate energy discussions everywhere. A week after my paddleboard adventure, a whitewater guide on Costa Rica's Rio Tenorio, in the country's northwest coastal area, described to me and a group of fellow rafters how his country's rivers had been harnessed beneficially to produce "clean energy" and clear the way to a nearly carbon-free future.

Costa Rica is now completing the largest hydropower dam in Central America, a project that will likely devastate the Reventazón River. The 426-foot-tall structure is being touted as a shining example of Costa Rica's commitment to the goals of the Kyoto Protocol, and the "Clean Development Mechanism," in particular. The methane emissions it will create do not appear to have been considered, and may never be measured. But as troubling as Costa Rica's situation may be, it represents just one small piece of an enormous global problem.

Dams are being built at a record pace all across the world. The Chinese government recently proposed to build the largest hydropower project in the world across the border in Tibet. Just one of the dams to be included would be three times the size of the current world-record-holder, Three Gorges Dam on the Yangtze River. Further, the conservation group International Rivers reports that, "Currently, no less than 3,700 hydropower projects are under construction or in the pipeline" across the planet.

Hydropower is dirty energy, and should be regarded just like fossil fuel. And environmentalists, far from embracing it, should be battling to shut down hydropower plants and block the arrival of new ones just as vigorously as we work to close and prevent construction of dirty coal plants.

At this critical moment in the planet's history, philanthropic funders that support action against climate change must fund a movement against hydropower. Unless the scientific truth about methane emissions from dams is more widely acknowledged, *pura vida* will never be achieved in Costa Rica or anywhere else.

--end--

Hydropower Will Undermine COP21 as 'False Solution' to Climate Change

(*EcoWatch*, November 2015)

"Big hydroelectric dams are a false solution because of the methane." —Randy Hayes, Oct. 8, 2015, Denver, Colorado

Over the past 15 years, the "methane problem" with hydropower has made minor blips in international news and has just begun to infiltrate the discussion of how it is wrong to use hydropower as a solution to fight climate change.

Hydropower is almost always greenwashed and sold to the public and policymakers as "clean energy" and "carbon-free."

The non-profit environmental group International Rivers has spearheaded much of the education and advocacy, and scientific journals as well as climate-related news sites like Climate Central are also taking up the case. Hydropower has been called a "methane factory" and "methane bomb" that is just beginning to rear its ugly head as a major source of greenhouse gas emissions that have so-far been unaccounted for in climate change discussions and analyses.

Scientific studies indicate that methane emissions from hydropower dams and reservoirs can vary dramatically. In northern subarctic climates, methane emissions have been measured as a small fraction of greenhouse gas emissions as compared to coal-fired power plants. In temperate climates like much of the U.S. and Europe, methane emission measurements vary by sub-climate, size of reservoir and vegetation growth, but have been measured from small to large as compared to the emissions from coal-fired power plants. In tropical environments, hydropower methane emissions have been measured as high as double those of the greenhouse emissions of a coal-fired power plant that generates the same amount of electricity.

Further, although the Intergovernmental Panel on Climate Change (IPCC) has guidelines on calculating methane emissions from hydropower dams/reservoirs, there have been very few measurements of these methane emissions at the same time that large hydropower projects are being built by the thousands across the planet. One Brazilian scientist estimates that methane from hydropower currently accounts for 23 percent of all human-caused worldwide methane emissions. As hydropower plants proliferate, that number will only increase.

Hydropower is almost always greenwashed and sold to the public and policymakers as "clean energy" and "carbon-free." Even though the IPCC lists hydropower's methane emissions as a greenhouse gas source, and over a decade of science refutes the claim that hydropower is clean energy, the myth of carbon-free hydropower is embedded in the Kyoto Protocol's "Clean Development Mechanism" to address planetary climate change and is increasingly being implemented by countries in attendance at COP 21 in Paris. Even worse, the World Bank still lists, promotes and funds hydropower as "clean energy," and nearly every country in the world is building hydropower plants under the same auspices. Even the U.S. government still perpetuates the anti-science myth of clean hydropower.

In the lead-up to COP 21, countries have been sending their "Intended Nationally Determined Contributions (INDCs)" to the United Nations. An INDC is a description of how each country intends to reduce its carbon emissions.

Let's look at five quick, random examples out of the 181 INDCs sent to the United Nations so far:

1. China is in the midst of building dozens of massive hydropower plants per year, including the largest on the planet. In its INDC, China states they intend to: "proactively promote the development of hydro power, on the premise of ecological and environmental protection and inhabitant resettlement."

2. India's INDC uses hydropower to meet its emission reduction target, and states: "With a vast potential of more than 100 GW, a number of policy initiatives and actions are being undertaken to aggressively pursue development of country's vast hydro-potential."

3. Japan's INDC states that it intends to reach its "emissions reduction target" in part by getting to nine percent hydropower by 2030. Japan has dozens of currently operating hydropower plants with dozens more in the planning stages.

4. Canada's INDC states that it will use "low-impact hydro" as one of its "investments to encourage the generation of electricity from renewable energy" Canada has dozens of new hydropower dams under construction, and few if any are even remotely considered "low-impact hydro."

5. Costa Rica's INDC boasts: "Costa Rica has a long standing tradition of innovation on hydroelectric generation, in conservation and specially, on matters of climate change." Costa Rica routinely markets itself as having a nearly carbon-free energy system, with more than 80 percent coming from hydropower—with absolutely none of the methane emissions measured or accounted for in its INDC—and is just finishing construction of the largest hydropower dam in Central America.

What's even more problematic is that many of the countries around the world that are most aggressively pursuing hydropower don't even list it in their INDC, but rather state they are using the 2006 IPCC Guidelines for National Greenhouse Gas Inventories to calculate their emissions and their reductions in emissions by using various energy types.

Take Indonesia as just one example, which has built and is continuing to build dozens of massive hydropower dams. In their INDC, Indonesia does not mention hydropower, stating that they will meet emissions reductions and that: "The inventory is based on 2006 IPCC Guideline for National Greenhouse Gas inventories."

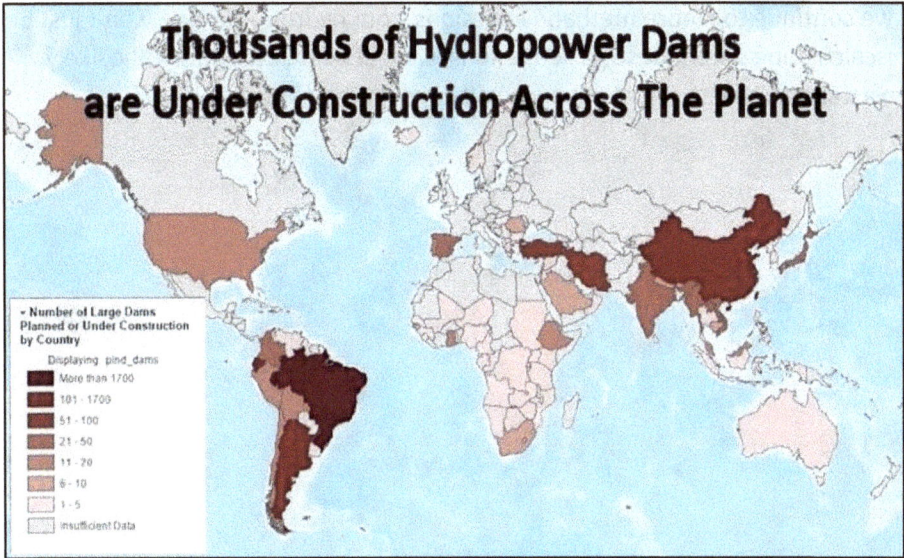

Thousands of Hydropower Dams are Under Construction Across The Planet

- Number of Large Dams Planned or Under Construction by Country

Displaying: plnd_dams

- More than 1700
- 101 - 1700
- 51 - 100
- 21 - 50
- 11 - 20
- 6 - 10
- 1 - 5
- Insufficient Data

I have deep skepticism about whether these countries are using the guidelines correctly, because even in 2006, the guidelines contained methane emissions calculations from dams and reservoirs, including the "CH4 [methane] Emissions From Flooded Lands" appendix to chapter four, which contains specific calculations for methane emissions upstream and downstream of dams. Thus, countries that are completely destroying their rivers and their climate with hydropower including Malaysia, Brazil, Guatemala, Russia and even the U.S. don't even list hydropower as a methane emissions source in their INDC, while including hydropower as a clean energy source, all under the auspices of likely misconstrued or purposely ignored IPCC guidelines.

How bad could it get? The Eastern European Balkan countries have recently announced they want to build 2,700 hydropower dams and every single one is being touted as a clean energy alternative to fight climate change.

As the world cartwheels towards COP 21, there are many reasons why scientists and advocates have little faith that the negotiations will yield consequential results to fight climate change. The lack of information about the methane emissions from hydropower, the apparent lack of enforcement of the IPCC guidelines and the ruse of calling hydropower "clean energy" are just more issues in the long list of problems with COP 21.

If we continue to ignore methane emissions from hydropower, we won't just be miscalculating greenhouse gas emissions, we will be miscalculating the likely devastating impacts climate change will have on the planet.

--end--

Part II: Saving The Colorado River

Disaster Capitalism on the Colorado River

(*USA Today*, March 2016)

Private sector has devastated the Colorado. Why will federal 'water moonshot' promote more destruction?

In December of 2015, the Obama administration, led by Interior Secretary Sally Jewell, announced that it was going to do a "**Moonshot for Water**." The press release and media reports around the announcement soared with rhetoric about how new "public-private partnerships" using "private sector investment" were going to save America's threatened and crumbling water systems from the massive threat of climate change. Much of the focus for this moonshot is on the Colorado River which has experienced a **15-year drought** and is poised to be in a state of worsening **climate-change induced drought** or worse as we head deep into the 21st century.

I'm very skeptical that this moonshot is going to save the river or us from climate change.

First, the private sector is already extremely involved in the complete draining and destruction of the Colorado River. The many federal government-built dams on the river pipe water almost exclusively to the private sector. About 70% of the water is drained out to supply agriculture and related interests; the other 30% or so goes to industry and cities, where it has helped fuel the massive real estate industry in southwestern U.S. states, including Southern California.

A 2015 study commissioned by a business group, Protect The Flows, stated that the Colorado River provides $1.4 trillion in economic activity every year for southwestern states. Further, much of this complete damming and destruction of the river since at least 1956 has been paid for by U.S. taxpayers, but in many cases, particularly agriculture, the federal government practically gives the water away to private interests through significant subsidies.

Second, while the Interior Department "Moonshot" press release contained a lot of rhetoric about how private sector investments would support water conservation, recycling and habitat protection, it also contained some very concerning language about "advanc(ing) efficient permitting" for projects, which could include "storage, pipelines, and canals." In light of some of Secretary Jewell's recent activities along the Colorado River basin, my concerns are amplified. In the last 24 months, Jewell's Bureau of Reclamation has approved a large new controversial diversion of water out of the Upper Colorado River; has pushed forward the permitting process for a controversial new diversion in New Mexico; and hasn't registered any objection to a massive new diversion in Wyoming. In addition, in Utah and Colorado, large new dams and diversions are in the permitting process by other arms of the federal government, but Jewell's Bureau of Reclamation has not registered any concern.

Third and finally, what sort of "private sector investment" is occurring now along the Colorado River and what might happen in the future? It's varied, but it contains some large-scale purchases of land and water by people and foreign governments that appear to be speculating that this increasingly scarce resource will be further depleted by climate change, causing its price to rise higher and higher. Over the past 24 months, foreign governments, including Saudi Arabia, have bought up farmland in Southern California and Arizona. McKenzie Funk, author of *Windfall: The Booming Business of Global Warming,* reports that hedge funds focusing on water have bought water rights in the Colorado River basin, and there's increasing talk about how private equity firms are popping up to buy and sell water throughout the Colorado River system.

People and firms that speculate in the increasing scarcity of water due to climate change like to call themselves, "climate change investors." But another phrase for this is "Disaster Capitalism," popularized by Naomi Klein's 2008 book, *The Shock Doctrine*: *The Rise of Disaster Capitalism*. Disaster capitalists troll around the world looking for ways to make enormous amounts of money when disasters strike. The 2015 book *Disaster Capitalism: Making A Killing Out Of Catastrophe* by Antony Loewenstein highlighted the wars, floods, famines and other climate-related catastrophes that have recently occurred across the planet and how capitalism swept in to get rich off of the doom and misery.

In conjunction with the "Moonshot for Water," the Obama administration is held a summit last week to discuss all of the innovative ideas that the public can submit for protecting and ensuring water supplies as climate change worsens. Here's my idea: Focus on the protection and restoration of the Colorado River ecosystem, and make sure that the river's amazing water resource is administered with equity and justice so that profiteering is minimized and the public good is maximized for all of the species — human and non-human alike — that depend on the river for survival.

--end--

Lake Powell: Going, Going, Gone?

(*EcoWatch*, August 2016)

The 16-year drought on the Colorado River has drained Lake Mead and Lake Powell to their combined lowest level in history. But that's nothing compared to what could happen, according to a new study from the State of Colorado.

The study indicates that a drought like the one that happened in 2000 – 2006 "would empty Lake Powell," according to the *Aspen Daily News.* "Another potential conclusion from the risk study is that any new trans-mountain diversion would only make it more likely that Powell would go below target levels," the publication noted.

And, whether you want to believe it or not, water agencies in Colorado, Wyoming and Utah are proposing to do just that. In fact, Denver Water, Northern Water (in Colorado), and the states of Wyoming and Utah are all proposing even more dams and diversions of water out of the river and its tributaries that would accelerate the draining of Lake Powell and cause serious legal consequences for the entire Southwest U.S.

Further, climate change scientists have painted a bullseye on the Southwest U.S., indicating that it will get hotter and drier, with even less flow into the

Colorado River. The lead investigator in the in-progress Colorado report has even said, "I haven't shown the climate change hydrology because it just scares everybody."

Save the Colorado has formally opposed all new proposed dams and diversions out of the river or its tributaries. We believe climate change is real and will have a serious impact on the Colorado River. The solution proposed by the State of Colorado is to buy massive amounts of water from farmers in Colorado, and then let that water run downstream to Lake Powell to keep the water level high enough to produce electricity at Glen Canyon Dam.

This plan is very unlikely to be successful. There's just not enough farmers who would want to sell massive amounts of water in order to keep the hydroelectric turbines spinning. Further, it could cost hundreds of millions of dollars every year to buy out those farmers even if they would sell.

What makes more sense is a responsible, planned effort by the government to drain Lake Powell, rather than letting drought and climate change do it in a haphazard way.

Lake Powell's days are numbered. The lake was a mistake, it's time to forsake.

--end--

Environmental Law Enforcement Helps Avert Shortage on the Colorado River

(*Save The Colorado*, August 2016)

News reports this week celebrated as the federal government announced that there would not be an official "shortage" on the Colorado River in 2016 or 2017 that would force California, Nevada, and Arizona to divert less water out of the river. Several journalists pointed to "water conservation" as the reason that this shortage was averted, and that is partially true. The lower basin states have made some good progress on their collaborative plan to take less water out of Lake Mead, thus helping to avert the shortage.

But what was completely missed in the news coverage was the role of good old-fashioned law enforcement by environmental groups to also help avert the shortage. Over the past five years, Save The Colorado has led or supported multiple law enforcement activities that helped keep dramatic amounts of water in the Colorado River. For example.

1. Flaming Gorge Pipeline: In 2013 and 2014, we helped lead a coalition of groups that enforced laws that helped stop the permitting process for this project that proposed to take 250,000 acre feet of water out of the Green River before it flows into the Colorado River.

2. Fontenelle Dam Re-Engineering: In 2015 and 2016 Save The Colorado has been bird-dogging this proposal by the State of Wyoming to divert a new 125,000 acre feet of water out of the Green River. Members of Congress are trying to move a bill that would allow WY to divert more water; Save The Colorado will be working to stop the project if it moves into the permitting process.

3. Moffat Collection System Project: Over the last few years, Save The Colorado has helped lead the fight to stop this Denver Water project as it moves through the permitting process with the Army Corps of Engineers. Proposing to take a new 15,000 acre feet out of the Colorado River, the project violates federal laws and would pour tens-of-thousands of tons of cement across South Boulder Creek in Boulder County, Colorado.

4. Windy Gap Firming Project: Over the last few years, Save The Colorado has led the fight to stop this disastrous project that proposes to divert a new 30,000 acre feet of water out of the Colorado River to slake the thirst of bluegrass lawns in Northern Colorado.

5. Gila River Diversion: Save The Colorado provided support to the groups in New Mexico that are fighting this proposed diversion of 12,000 acre feet of water out of the Gila River before it flows into Arizona and meets the Colorado River. As the project moves through the permitting process, we will stand by to support our New Mexico colleagues again.

6. Lake Powell Pipeline: Save The Colorado has supported and joined a broad coalition of groups in Utah to help stop this proposed project that would take a new 86,000 acre feet of water out of the Colorado River. As the project moves through the permitting process, we will be joining our Utah colleagues, locking arms to protect the river and stop this project.

7. Green River Nuclear Power Plant: Save The Colorado has provided support to HEAL UTAH and other groups in Utah that are fighting this project that proposes to divert a new 53,000 acre feet of water out of the Green River.

8. Colorado Water Plan: We've also bird-dogged several additional proposals including large new diversions that are being discussed in the Colorado Water Plan process.

Americans are very lucky. In the 1960s and 1970s our forefathers and foremothers in Congress had the extraordinary vision to create and pass exceptional environmental laws to protect the public's health and environment. Those laws — including the National Environmental Policy Act, Clean Water Act, and Endangered Species Act — gave the public not just the right, but the responsibility, to enforce the law as these types of water projects move through the permitting process. Further, if we the public believe that the federal government has broken the law, Congress gave us the right and responsibility to enforce the law in federal court.

By bird-dogging every one of these projects through the permitting process, Save The Colorado is proud to be a law-enforcement organization as our forefathers and foremothers envisioned. We intend to continue our law enforcement activities as long as the laws continue to be threatened or broken.

Yes, a shortage on the Colorado River was averted in 2016 and 2017. But, let's tell the whole story — if every project above would have been permitted and built, at least another 500,000 acre feet of water (that's 162 billion gallons, equaling 5 feet of water in Lake Mead, *every year*) would have been diverted out of the river and not flowed into Lake Powell and potentially Lake Mead. The facts are clear: Environmental law enforcement helps avert a shortage on the Colorado River.

--end--

While the Animas River spill is eye-catching, Western rivers face an even bigger threat

(High Country News, August 2015)

If there's any good news to be gained from the toxic spill of mine wastes into the Animas River upstream of Durango, Colorado, it's that public attention has suddenly shifted to the health of rivers in the West.

The 3-million-gallon accident riveted the media, even rating a story in England's Guardian newspaper. Here at home, officials took action almost immediately: Biologists put out fish cages to see if the sludge was killing fish, and chemists began testing the murky water for acidity and heavy metal concentrations. Within a few days, the governor of Colorado, both Colorado U.S. senators, and the administrator of the Environmental Protection Agency -- whose contractors triggered the spill -- showed up in Durango to express their regret, outrage, support, etc. They promised that it would never happen again.

But of course a disaster is sure to occur again, because there are thousands of century-old abandoned mines in the region that have never been thoroughly cleaned up. And as the saying goes: Acid mine drainage is forever.

But while an orange plume of heavy metals moving through a river system toward a major reservoir like Lake Powell is certainly a serious problem, there's another danger targeting rivers in the West. It's the kind of disaster that sometimes kills every living creature in a river, imperils the river's health for weeks and months, causes extensive contaminations of e. coli and heavy metals, and destroys the recreational economy — rafting, tubing, fishing -- for months at a time.

This disaster is caused by dams. Whether they are large or small, they block a river so that water can be diverted for farms, ranches or domestic use. From its beginnings high on the Continental Divide, for example, the Colorado River loses 90 percent of its flow to diversion in the first 40 miles.

Once the Arkansas River leaves the mountains and heads for Kansas, it becomes a dribble of its former self. The dammed and diverted South Platte River through Denver is often a putrid, algae-ridden and depleted mess, and when it exits town, most of its flow is made up of discharge from Denver's sewage treatment plant.

The Cache la Poudre, near my home in northern Colorado, is sometimes drained bone-dry as it moves through downtown Fort Collins, and when it does have water in it, its native flow is diminished over 50 percent by dams and diversions.

Colorado is just the tip of the iceberg of river destruction. Rivers across New Mexico and Utah are in a similar desperate condition. And in Southern California and Arizona, most rivers are drained completely dry every single year. The Gila River in Arizona, once a large and beautiful tributary of the Colorado River, is now completely dead except during rare monsoon rains that fall perhaps once every 20 years.

But there's worse to come. The states of Colorado, Wyoming, New Mexico and Utah have all just gone through official water-planning processes and are proposing even more dams and river-draining activity. The governor of Wyoming has called for "10 new dams in 10 years." The state of Utah wants to put "a dam on every river in the state," and water agencies in Colorado are proposing large new diversions out of the Colorado River. In addition, Colorado yearns to retain every legal drop before its rivers cross the state's boundaries.

As you watch the media focus for a while on river health, consider this trivia question: Where was the last major dam and river-destroying project in Colorado?

If you guessed it was on the Animas River, southwest of Durango, you're right. The controversial Animas-La Plata Project erected a huge, new dam and reservoir, a pumping station to divert water out of the Animas River, and the federal government did it all with virtually no mitigation to offset the impacts to the river.

Were elected officials outraged at this project? No, they celebrated it and named the reservoir Lake Nighthorse after former Colorado Sen. Ben Nighthorse Campbell.

If this plume of poisoned water moving downstream teaches us anything, maybe it ought to be this: All of our rivers are at risk so long as we continue to prevent them from running free.

--end--

This Is What Epic Drought Looks Like: Lake Mead Hits Historic Low

(*EcoWatch*, April 2015)

The big doom-and-gloom news in the water world this week is that America's former largest reservoir, Lake Mead near Las Vegas on the Colorado River, hit a historic low on Sunday. The reservoir serves water to the states of Arizona, Nevada and California, providing sustenance to nearly 20 million people and crops that feed the nation.

All the news stories and pundits blame the historic draining of Lake Mead on drought and/or climate change, but I'm going to take a different tack on this story. The reservoir hit a historic low because the entire Colorado River water supply system has been grossly mismanaged. Further, the gross mismanagement is escalating as the upstream states plot their next moves to further drain the reservoirs imperiling the economy of the region as well as degrading the health of the Colorado River.

For nearly two decades every water supply agency in the Southwest U.S., including the U.S. Bureau of Reclamation which manages the Colorado River system, has known that the river is "over-allocated"—i.e., that more water is taken out than flows in. Yet, almost nothing has been done to stem the decline which is likely to get worse as climate change progresses. Finally in 2013, the Bureau of Reclamation publicly created the "Colorado River Basin Study" that, sure enough, said the system is in severe decline and offered a bunch of ideas on how to address it. However, few of those ideas have been enacted as the nation watches the reservoir drop and Nevada, Arizona and California still take almost all of their full allotment of water out of the river.

Even more malevolently, the level of water in Lake Mead is partly driven by how much water flows into it from the upstream states of Colorado, Utah and Wyoming. At the same time that Mead hit a historic low, those three states are not only still taking all of the same water out of the system, they are aggressively planning to build even more dams and reservoirs that divert more water.

- In Colorado, Denver Water is proposing to build a larger dam/reservoir, Northern Water (which supplies water to Northern Colorado) is also proposing to build a new reservoir, and the State of Colorado is going through a planning process to build billions of dollars worth of water projects, all of which would further drain the Colorado River ecosystem.

- In Utah, state and local planners are moving forward with a massive pipeline proposal out of the Colorado River at Lake Powell, and the state government is going through a planning process that proposes to put more dams on every river in the state.

- In Wyoming, water planners are aggressively trying to start two reservoir projects that would further drain the Green River which flows into the Colorado, and are planning more water diversion projects in the future.

All of these projects are being proposed so the upstream states can get the last legally allowed drops of water out of the system before it collapses in the near future. This water management is a kind of "Mutually Assured Destruction" escalating the water war across the Southwest U.S.

If there is a slight bright side here it's that the states have agreed to some "trigger" points in Lake Mead—levels to which if the reservoir drops, the states will start taking out less water, led first by Arizona. Those triggers will likely be hit in the next 12 to 18 months. Further, water agencies in Nevada,

Arizona and Southern California have also agreed to some new conservation measures that will take less water out of the reservoir.

But that's not enough. Here's the bold action that needs to be taken:

1.   Every water supply agency needs to agree to water conservation measures that stabilize the system right now, before it reaches trigger points and collapse scenarios. The conservation measures should occur in cities and on farms across the Southwest U.S. If the water supply agencies won't do it, the federal government—which has the authority—needs to step in and get it done.

2.   No water supply agency should propose to take one more new drop of water out of the Colorado River system. Instead of Mutually Assured Destruction, we need Multi-Lateral Disarmament. All of the proposed projects should be stopped—if the agencies won't stop them, then the federal government should. If the federal government won't do it, then the court system should as these project go through permitting processes and get hit with inevitable lawsuits.

3.   The health of the Colorado River needs to be addressed for the first time in history. At the top of the system in Colorado, the river is nearly drained and even more endangered by proposed dam projects. In the middle section of the river in Utah and Arizona, the dams have completely degraded the ecosystem leading to multiple endangered fish and a massively disrupted flow regime and ecology. At the bottom of the system, the Colorado River is still drained bone dry—all 5 trillion gallons drained out before it reaches the Gulf of California creating a holocaust of environmental degradation.

Gross mismanagement needs to be replaced with bold action, and then the doom and gloom news stories would be replaced with hope for a brighter future.

--end--

Is Las Vegas Betting the Colorado River Will Go Dry?

(*High Country News*, August 2014)

Las Vegas is a city that plays the odds, and if you want to know which odds to play, you need to follow the smart money. Unfortunately, that money seems to be moving toward building yet more dams that will drain yet more water out of an already oversubscribed Colorado River.

Unlike most cities in the Southwest U.S., Las Vegas depends completely on the Colorado River. If the river goes dry, Vegas goes dry, and so how the river is managed by the states upstream of Vegas will partly define the city's fate. The Colorado River already has more water taken out of it than flows into it, and Lake Mead -- from which Vegas gets its Colorado River water -- is less than half full and dropping farther every year.

If we want to predict the future of the Colorado River, we can take a look at how the players around the Colorado River Basin plan to spend their money, especially the states of Wyoming, Colorado, New Mexico and Utah.

Wyoming recently went through a planning process in which the state decided that it needs "more dams." It's now planning to spend hundreds of millions of dollars, if not billions, to get more water out of Wyoming's rivers, including the Green River, which feeds the Colorado.

Colorado is going through a "Water Plan" process right now that includes a discussion about taking more water out of the Colorado River and other rivers in the state, at an estimated cost of at least a billion dollars.

New Mexico just OK'd the Gila River Pipeline, a proposal to potentially spend up to a billion dollars to get more water out of the Gila, which flows into the Colorado River downstream. And Utah just went through a water-planning process where it proposes to spend up to $15 billion on new water-supply projects that would include taking water out of the Colorado River system. A high-ranking state official said, "It is necessary to put dams on all rivers in Utah."

The folks downstream in Arizona and California are paying keen attention. In Arizona, most of the Colorado River water flows through the vast Central Arizona Project, whose director recently said, "It's becoming increasingly likely we'll see a shortage declared in 2017." In a similar tone, the Metropolitan Water District of Southern California, which gets half of its water from the Colorado River and is facing the worst drought in the state's history, also recently warned about upcoming shortages.

Some back-of-the-envelope math puts the money these states are wagering on water at around $20 billion, all of which would further drain the Colorado River. On the other side of the equation, it's absolutely true that all of these states, as well as their major cities and water districts, will spend hundreds of millions of dollars in water conservation and efficiency programs to lower their demand.

Las Vegas claims it's spent $200 million over the past 15 years on not using water. What's more, in the past year we've seen the first significant step to restore the Colorado River. Four large water districts (including Las Vegas) and the U.S. Bureau of Reclamation propose to invest "up to $11 million" in a "Colorado River System Conservation Program" that would work to keep more water in the river and Lake Mead.

But if we look at the smart money in Las Vegas, something else is going on. Las Vegas' Southern Nevada Water Authority is frantically drilling the "Third Straw" under Lake Mead at a cost of $850 million, racing to get its water out of the draining lake before it's too late. And just two weeks ago, the Southern Nevada Water Authority recommended spending another $650 million on a new pumping station, just in case Lake Mead hits "Dead Pool."

That's $1.5 *billion* to plan for a worst-case scenario -- the death of the Colorado River. In comparison, Las Vegas' Water Authority is investing just a few *million* in the Colorado River System Conservation Program to keep the river flowing.

From Dec. 10-14, the Colorado River Water Users Association will hold its annual conference. The group is made up of all the states and cities and farmers in the entire Southwest; they amicably describe themselves as the "water buffaloes." The theme of the conference is "Challenged But Unbroken: Sustaining the Colorado River." Fittingly, the conference is set for Las Vegas, where everyone plays the odds for a living.

--end--

Stop the War Against the Colorado River

(*EcoWatch*, January 2015)

"Disarmament, with mutual honor and confidence, is a continuing imperative." —Dwight D. Eisenhower

As we head into 2015, the health of Colorado River is at extreme risk as is the economies of states in the lower part of the river in Arizona, Nevada and California that depend on flows in the river. Drought continues in the Southwest U.S., climate change is predicted to decrease river flows an additional 10 to 30 percent, and the level of Lake Mead—the reservoir that holds water for much of Nevada, Arizona and Southern California—continues to fall with no end in sight.

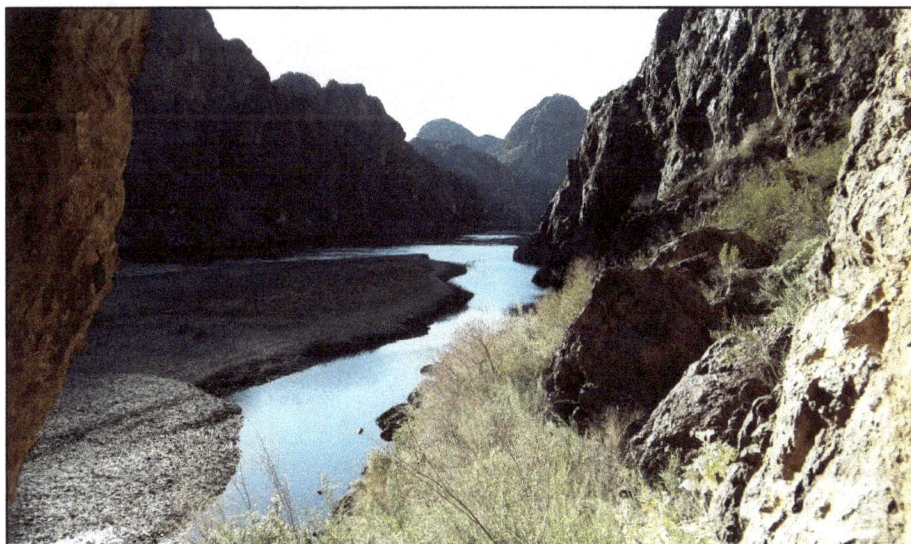

2014 saw one important event in Colorado River management to address these issues—a historic agreement between water agencies in the three states noted above to dramatically escalate their conservation and water-sharing programs. But this won't be enough to stave off the continually falling levels of Lake Mead. Further, and even worse, the biggest threat to the Colorado River is coming from the upstream states—Utah, Colorado, Wyoming and New Mexico are proposing to take even more water out of the river.

Specifically, in recent water planning processes in the upstream states, Colorado proposed $20 billion worth of dam and reservoir projects, Utah proposed $15 billion, Wyoming proposed "10 dams in 10 years" and New Mexico endorsed a bill-dollar water project, most of which in all four states would take even more water out of the Colorado River before it gets to Lake Mead.

Statements made by water officials in the upstream states highlight this escalating water war. Colorado's lead water official recently said, "If anybody thought we were going to roll over and say, 'OK, California, you're in a really bad drought, you get to use the water that we were going to use,' they're mistaken." And the lead water official in Utah recently stated, "It's necessary to put dams on all rivers in Utah." Thus, the upstream states have declared war on the river and war against the downstream states.

We need multilateral disarmament on the Colorado River.

The health of the river including its endangered fish and vast recreational economy cannot support more diversions, nor can Lake Mead and the water supply needs of the downstream states. All told, the Colorado River has about 5 trillion gallons flowing in it in an average year. People—farms, cities, industries from Denver to Los Angeles and beyond—take out every single drop such that the river no longer reaches the Gulf of California. The upstream states may think they are legally entitled to more water out of the river, but common sense and environmental stewardship dictate otherwise.

The Colorado River is a patient in the emergency room. If the patient is bleeding out, you don't cut open a new artery to heal it, and that's what the proposed projects by the upstream states would do.

Just like how multilateral nuclear disarmament is the only sane and responsible policy to address our political wars, multilateral river disarmament is the only sane and responsible water policy for the states in the Colorado River basin in 2015.

Colorado, Utah, Wyoming and New Mexico need to put their water engineers on other types of work—instead of building more dams that destroy the river, a new water ethic that focuses on conservation and river health must move forward.

--end--

Can Climate Action Plans Combat Megadrought and Save the Colorado River?

(*EcoWatch*, March 2015)

If a city's water supply is threatened by climate change, should that city enact a strong climate action plan? I believe the answer is yes, but few cities throughout the Colorado River basin are moving forward aggressively to address climate change even though the threat is increasing every year.

Two of the largest reservoirs in the U.S.—Lakes Mead and Powell along the Colorado River—continue to lose water and are now less than half full with no prediction that the trend will change direction. The U.S. Bureau of Reclamation, which manages the reservoirs, and many scientific studies by independent researchers have reached the same conclusion: human overuse of the river and the likely impacts of climate change could have a profound negative impact on the amount of water flowing down the Colorado River and its ability to supply water for 40 million people.

A recent newspaper article discussing this issue was titled, "Climate change or just bad luck?" In the last 15 years, about 20 percent less water has flowed in the river compared to the 40 years prior. This river flow, which comes from snow falling in the Rocky Mountains in Colorado, Utah and Wyoming, is at historic lows already. Climate change is predicted to lower the snow and river flows by 8.5 percent or more. A recent study by the National Oceanographic and Atmospheric Administration used the term "megadrought" to describe what could be coming for the Colorado River basin if climate change is not abated.

In this quagmire, several cities in the Southwest U.S. that use water out of the Colorado River are enacting "Climate Action Plans" to reduce their carbon emissions. A few of those plans are highly ambitious and propose to reduce carbon emissions to zero. Several others have less lofty goals but are moving in the right direction. Here's a quick summary of some of the cities' plans in the seven Colorado River basin states:

Colorado: Several cities have aggressive plans including Fort Collins, Boulder and Aspen.

- Fort Collins proposes to get to 100 percent renewables by 2050.

- Aspen proposes an 80 percent reduction in greenhouse gas emissions by 2050.

- Boulder enacted a "climate action plan tax," and is in the process of "municipalizing" its utility to achieve an 80 percent reduction in greenhouse gas emissions by 2050.

- Denver's plan to reduce emissions is minimal, but the city has embarked on a lengthy "Climate Adaptation Plan."

Utah:

- Salt Lake City has proposed an 80 percent reduction in greenhouse gas emissions by 2050.

New Mexico:

- Albuquerque has proposed an 80 percent reduction in greenhouse gas emissions by 2050.

- Santa Fe recently created a "Climate Action Task Force" but has not yet to proposed emissions goals.

Wyoming:

- No traceable climate action plans are occurring in the Colorado River basin area of this heavy oil, gas and coal extraction state.

Nevada:

- Las Vegas is likely one of the first cities that may be hit by the impacts of climate change as the water levels in Lake Mead continue to drop. The city has committed to a smaller 30 percent reduction in its carbon footprint by 2030.

Arizona:

- Phoenix set a small goal of a 5 percent reduction by 2015 and achieved it. In 2011 Tucson signed on to the U.S. Mayors' Climate Protection Agreement (MCPA) goal of a 7 percent reduction by 2012.

Southern California:

- San Diego has an ambitious goal of 100 percent renewable energy by 2035. Los Angeles has a goal of a 35 percent reduction by 2030.

In addition to these cities, a number of cities across the basin and especially in Southern California signed on to the MCPA goal for a 7 percent reduction by 2012.

The Southwest U.S. has much to lose as climate change continues its grip and escalates across the basin. The list above is a cursory summary—local groups and governments likely have far more detail—but this post should help begin a broader discussion about the role cities can play in the climate-water nexus across the Colorado River basin. If "megadrought" is on the horizon, the leadership in cities like Boulder, Fort Collins and San Diego show that a "mega-response" is the smart path forward.

--end--

Colorado River and Sea of Cortez finally embrace after 20 years apart

(High Country News, May 2014)

They kissed. Like two long-lost lovers who had been cruelly kept apart for 20 years, the Colorado River and the Sea of Cortez finally embraced. The historic reunion occurred this May as the United States and Mexico worked together to restore the Colorado River Delta.

The "pulse flow" of water raced down from Lake Mead, boiled over Morelos Dam at the border and gently flooded the bone-dry Colorado River Delta. Overhead, a helicopter followed the journey, a photographer recording the historic mingling.

Our messy human concoctions of cities, farms and power plants had drained the river dry, so it took human intervention to return some water to the lower river. If the damming of the Colorado River and draining of the Delta symbolized the failure of the North American environmental movement, this attempt at restoration symbolizes the exact opposite. Yet the job has only just begun, as the pulse flow to bring the Delta to life has ended, and the hard work of buying more water begins.

Our untidy and complicated arrangements are still at work up and down the entire Colorado River. At the very same moment in history when we are working hard to find ways to restore the Delta, almost every state and local agency is determined to drain even more water from the river:

Denver Water is trying to get more water out of the Colorado for the "Moffat Project" and pipe it through the Continental Divide and down into the city.

"Northern Water," another agency in northern Colorado, is trying to build the "Windy Gap Firming Project" to do the same thing.

The state of Colorado is creating a "Colorado Water Plan" in which the Front Range Water Council, a coalition of agencies from Greeley to Denver to Colorado Springs, has proposed a massive new "Trans Mountain Diversion" from the Colorado River.

Wyoming is considering the same thing, holding meetings and making plans, through a process called the "Wyoming Water Strategy."

Utah is equally brazen, developing a "State Water Strategy," and proposing both a massive pipeline out of Lake Powell and a new "Green River Nuclear Power Plant," each of which would further drain the Colorado River and its tributaries.

And New Mexico, not to be left out, has proposed a "Gila River Pipeline" that would drain more water out of the Gila, nearly ensuring it would never again flow into the Colorado River.

Everyone's trying to capture the last legally allowed drop. And, of course, climate change has entered the fray with its own agenda, which may topple all of our schemes. Yet I am optimistic.

A few weeks ago, I stood in the Delta and watched the Colorado River crawl toward me through the sand. A small team of us had walked a mile to see the river emerge, and when it happened I was speechless. As the water edged to my toes, it felt cool as it engulfed my feet even though it had traveled miles over 100-degree desert sand. It almost smelled like the snow-capped Colorado mountains that I'd flown over just the day before.

As the Colorado River kissed the Sea of Cortez, I felt it suffuse the environmental community with a sense of hope and passion. Social media of the event quickly came alive with photos and posts that went viral, the mainstream media covered the story for days afterwards, and river lovers felt they'd scored a rare victory.

There's no denying that environmental advocates are an odd breed. We fight the apocalypse every day and we almost never win, and in the end few of us even expect to. Pessimism becomes a way of life. So whenever a victory is scored, it buoys our hopes. Give us an inch, we'll run for a mile. Give us a little shot of hope, and we'll fight for years in the trenches. There's an amazing amount of work to do to further protect and restore the Colorado River, and there's an amazing cadre of people lined up to do it.

So if you are involved with Denver Water, or Northern Water, or are part of an organization proposing yet another dam or pipeline, you should consider what you're up against. You have "plans" and "strategies," you have sprawling suburbs and Chambers of Commerce demanding more water. You have elected officials spouting off about the need for growth.

What do we have? Hopes, dreams, passions and lawyers, and a river that has once again met its sea. A long-overdue and beautiful reunion — sealed with a kiss.

--end--

Obituary for a river? Not if we start fighting

(*Boulder Weekly*, July 2014)

"Silence is a political stance. It defends the status quo." – Lee Camp

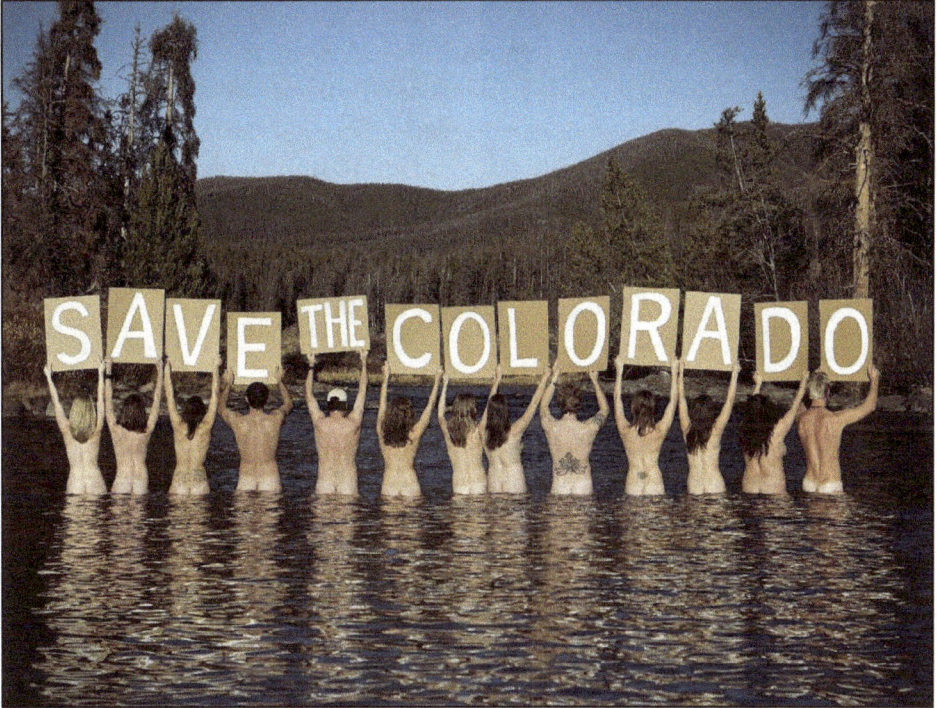

When I read "Obituary For A River" in the *Boulder Weekly* last week, I was surprised at the disempowerment and parochialism displayed by the various people interviewed in this article. My goodness — what a depressing story! That's why I want to introduce you to the vaquita.

The vaquita is the most endangered cetacean (whale species) in the world — it's a beautiful and very small porpoise that lives in the Gulf of California where the Colorado River no longer meets the sea. Scientists estimate that only about 200 vaquita are still alive, and that it is increasingly threatened with extinction every year. One of its possible threats is because there are no freshwater and nutrients flowing into the Gulf, due to the damming and draining of the Colorado River from its headwaters in Grand County, Colorado, all the way to the City of Los Angeles.

And so when we talk about the rivers of Colorado, including the Fraser River which was the subject of this article, we are not just talking about short-term or very localized issues, we are talking about people and endangered wildlife throughout the Southwest U.S. from Denver to Mexicali and the Gulf of California.

The single biggest threat to every one of these rivers and the wildlife they support is new proposed dams and diversions, like Denver Water's "Moffat Collect System Project." And the single biggest thing you can do to address these threats is to stand up, speak out, and fight to stop the projects. Here's what you need to know:

First, several people in the article said that "Denver owns the water," and thus that Denver can and should divert the water and thereby has the right to kill this river. That is not accurate.

Water in the state of Colorado is owned by the public, and through a system of laws we the people grant "rights" to use that water to cities, farmers and industries. In so doing, we stipulate how they must use this water in a rightful manner. For example, they can't waste it or use it for a purpose that is not beneficial, and when they propose dams and pipelines to divert it out of rivers, they have to comply with a broad array of federal, state, and local laws including the National Environmental Policy Act, Clean Water Act and Endangered Species Act.

Those three laws, and others at the state and local level, are part of the backbone of our democracy, and when congress passed those laws, they also gave we the people the right to enforce those laws for the future benefit of people and non-human critters we share this planet with.

Second, the problems with the Moffat Project and the Fraser River are not just limited to the people of Grand County as was suggested in the article. Other people and groups have a stake in this issue:

> • As this newspaper has previously reported, the Moffat Project will dramatically and negatively impact the people of Boulder County — it is a massive dam enlargement and would be the biggest construction project in the county's history. The people of Boulder County have extraordinary legal power to decide what happens in their county and have the right to exercise it.

• The project will primarily support wasteful water use and lawn watering in the metro Denver area, both of which represent bad water policy by one of the most high-profile water agencies in the American West. Our organization — the Save The Colorado River Campaign — and others have spent years promoting alternatives to these projects, including conservation, efficiency, recycling, better growth management, and cooperative agreements with farmers. Federal and state laws require that those alternatives be considered and evaluated when dams are proposed.

• If Denver gets to set a precedent of completely killing a river, then every city in the Colorado River basin (the entire Southwest U.S.) will see that as an example of not only how to act, but of how the public — including environmental groups — will respond. The people of the West Slope of Colorado and conservation groups throughout the Southwest have the right to respond differently, to exercise their voices and the political will to address this threat.

Finally, there's an underlying feeling in this "obituary" of extraordinary disempowerment, and even more surprising is that it comes from the West Slope of Colorado, which is partly a libertarian bastion of the American West. Does Grand County have the Stockholm Syndrome? Conversely, not too far downstream in western Colorado there's a very different and more empowered discussion about a "Not One More Drop" campaign, meaning that some folks in Glenwood Springs, Grand Junction and farther west don't want one more drop of their rivers diverted over to Denver and the Front Range. The folks in Grand County ought to look west, not east to Denver, to solve their problem — spirited voices to save the rivers of western Colorado are alive and well downstream.

Which brings me back to the vaquita.

What an amazing little critter. Cute, shy, nearly extinct, and completely voiceless without our help. Whether these rivers live or die, whether this little porpoise lives or dies, is up to us. We need to unite together from the Front Range to the West Slope, and downstream to the Gulf of California, to keep our rivers, our culture, and our wildlife alive.

--end--

Drought Drains Lake Mead to Lowest Level as Nevada Senator Calls for Government Audit

(*EcoWatch*, July 2014)

As the largest reservoir in the U.S. falls to its lowest water level in history, Nevada State Sen. Tick Segerblom introduced a bill title and issued a press release on July 8 calling for an "independent scientific and economic audit of the Bureau of Reclamation's strategies for Colorado River management."

Sen. Segerblom's position represents the growing political impatience with the current management system for the river. He takes hard aim at the Bureau of Reclamation as being responsible for these problems as he says, "Reclamation may have played a major role in erecting our Colorado River infrastructure, but it's clearly time for people across the basin to begin leading its future management."

Lake Mead Hits Lowest Level in History

Further, the Senator calls for a more environmentally minded management focus on the health of the river as stated in his press release: "Healthy rivers signal healthy societies, yet Reclamation failed to mention ecological issues in its recent analysis. The Colorado River is a river of national parks, but the river running through them is struggling."

This week's history-making, bad-news event at Lake Mead has already triggered lots of news stories, but almost all of these stories focus on the water supply for Las Vegas, Phoenix and California. But what about the health of the river itself? Senator Segerblom's press release reminds us that this river is more than just water supply for cities and farms—it's a living entity full of species that depend on the river for survival, and as the lake level falls, the first entity to feel even more pain won't be Las Vegas or Phoenix but rather the river itself.

Let's take a look at the environmental problems with the Colorado River and how they are getting worse. Grab a cup of coffee because this is a buzzkill:

- Four federally listed endangered fish continue to struggle to survive in the Colorado River, but managers' answer to this problem is to continually spawn and restock the fish, not to address the underlying problem of too many dams and diversions.

- Many of the tributaries flowing into the Colorado River are severely depleted, and some, like the Gila River in Arizona, are completely drained dry almost every year.

- The ecological health of the Grand Canyon is severely degraded and imperiled—what was once a wild and brown frothy foment of a river filled with native fish, canyon-carving sediment and warm-water organisms is now a cold, clear-green, somewhat sterile and completely controlled dam/drainage system that has not been adequately mitigated or fixed.

- Climate change models indicate the decrease in flow in the Colorado River could be significantly more than Bureau of Reclamation is planning for, yet mangers have not even grappled with the last 15 years of drought let alone what climate change may increasingly offer.

- As river flows drop, as lake levels drop, and as climate change models indicate worsening conditions, cities and water districts in Colorado, Wyoming, Utah, New Mexico and Arizona are proposing even more dams and diversions out of the Colorado River system. All the states and the cities are trying to get the last legally allowed drop of water out of the river before someone else does.

- Almost 1/12 of the entire flow of the Colorado River simply evaporates into thin air or seeps away into the ground surrounding all of the reservoirs, yet the river's managers are not considering ways to mitigate or fix this loss to water supplies as well as to river health from the 50 to 100-year old dam and reservoir system.

To address these problems as well as water supply threats, the Bureau of Reclamation spent years creating the *Colorado River Basin Study* and released it publicly in 2012 with much fanfare. Since that time, Reclamation has appointed several "Working Groups" to further study the problem and offer solutions—including a "Healthy Flows Working Group"—but over a year has passed without public communication about recommendations or solutions.

To be fair, it's not completely all bad news—there are a few glimmers of hope around the Colorado River basin too. The effort by the Bureau to restore the Colorado River Delta has been positive, environmental groups' work to stop and stall new water projects has made a difference, and a few cities' new pilot project, Colorado River System Conservation Program, offers a potential path forward.

But despite these glimmers of hope, there's one overwhelming fact in the Colorado River ecosystem and it's painted bright white with the increasing size of the bathtub ring across the walls of Lake Mead—we are draining more water out of the system than the river is putting in.

Whether you agree or disagree with Sen. Segerblom's approach, something needs to change to address the water supply threats, and something must change as soon as possible to arrest the continual decline of the health of the Colorado River. The system, and the health of the river itself, cannot be sustained the way it's currently operated.

--end--

Will the Colorado River Get Fracked?

(*EcoWatch*, May 2013)

Two months ago a story started 'leaking' out of Western Colorado about a fracked-gas pipeline break—loaded with cancer-causing benzene—with fluids heading toward and eventually into Parachute Creek which is a tributary to the Colorado River. As water wells close to the Creek started testing positive for benzene, and then as the Creek itself tested positive for benzene above drinking water standards, the news media started telling a story of how the Colorado River—a drinking water source for 35 million people across the Southwest U.S.—was threatened. As of this writing the leak is still not cleaned up and the creek is still testing positive for benzene.

This one leak may be the tip of the iceberg for fracking impacts in the Colorado River basin.

Across the Colorado River basin in Colorado, Wyoming, New Mexico, Utah and in Southern California, a huge boom in natural gas and oil exploration and drilling—all using the extremely dangerous and controversial extraction method of fracking—is taking place that is increasingly imperiling water resources. Fracking has these impacts on water resources:

1. Fracking uses enormous amounts of water.

2. Fracking uses cancer-causing chemicals.

3. "Spills and releases" of drilling and fracking fluids on the ground are commonplace during the drilling and fracking stage of each well.

4. Unless wells are drilled and fracked properly, chemicals can leak into surrounding groundwater. Even when wells are drilled and fracked to the highest standards, there's no guarantee that cement casings around wells can't break and leak over time.

5. After the drilling and fracking process, there's no guarantee that fluids injected into the well can't migrate up into groundwater through geological fissures and cracks.

6. Millions of gallons of waste products from each fracked well are so badly poisoned with cancer-causing chemicals that the water is never purified and returned to rivers and streams, and instead is usually injected into even deeper aquifers and wells where government regulating agencies hope it stays forever.

More than a hundred thousand active oil and gas wells in the Colorado River already exist, and approximately a hundred thousand new wells—all to be fracked—are proposed. Many of these existing wells are near streams that connect to the Colorado River and some are right beside the Colorado River, and all of the proposed wells are in the same locations. Billions of gallons of toxic water and waste products have already been injected into deep disposal wells across the Colorado River basin every year, and billions more are proposed. Cancer-causing fracking chemicals are sometimes stored in tanks and open pits on the surface right beside rivers, including the Colorado River.

Here's a quick summary of drilling and fracking activity in the Colorado River basin:

Wyoming: Wyoming has thousands of oil and gas wells in and around the Colorado River headwaters of the Green River, and is planning for thousands more. Wyoming is home to one of the most famous and controversial cases of groundwater contamination due to fracking and drilling, in Pavillion in the southwestern part of the state, and is also known to have worse drilling-related air quality than Los Angeles. Drilling has decimated the landscape in the Green River valley, seriously impacting water runoff and wildlife habitat.

Colorado: Colorado's growing population has already stretched water supplies thin, but fracking is on track to help drain the last legally allowed drops of water out of the Colorado River's headwaters. Colorado currently has more than 40,000 active oil and gas wells, and is planning for up to 100,000— although many of those are on the Front Range, Colorado River water is piped under and across the Continental Divide to serve those wells, as well as to serve the thousands of wells in the Western part of the state in the Colorado River basin. About 60 percent of all waste is injected into deep disposal wells, and thousands of "spills and releases" have impacted groundwater and surface water throughout the state. Two Colorado cities have banned fracking and over a dozen have placed a moratorium on fracking.

Utah: All of the same drilling and fracking chaos in Colorado and Wyoming has also occurred in Utah which has been on a "fracking frenzy," with plans for thousands of more wells, many in the Colorado River basin, and some near and right beside the Colorado River on vast swaths of publicly owned land. Some of the ground-breaking science around climate-change causing methane leakage has occurred in Utah which currently has 11,000 producing oil and gas wells statewide.

New Mexico: New Mexico has more than 50,000 oil and gas wells and is drilling about 1,500 new wells per year, most of them fracked and the majority of which are in the Colorado River basin in northwest New Mexico. Industry spokespeople say New Mexico is in the "early stage of the shale play" as new hydraulic fracking technology has opened up hundreds of thousands of acres of public land for exploration and drilling. Of note, a bill was just killed in the state legislature to ban fracking, and Mora County New Mexico just recently passed a ban on fracking.

Nevada: Almost all of Nevada is outside of the Colorado River basin and there's currently only about 1,000 active oil and gas wells in the state, so fracking is not a huge issue for Nevada as it relates to the Colorado River. However in the northern part of the state, fracking proposals are moving forward, and because Nevada is a very parched state with internal water wars between Las Vegas and areas to the north, it is unpredictable how fracking could play out.

Arizona: There are very few active oil and gas wells in Arizona, almost no new prospecting, and virtually no fracking at this time.

California: California's current and future fracking potential is huge with more than 50,000 active oil and gas wells (mostly oil) and potential for "major shale oil plays" in the Monterey Shale adding up to 28,000 new wells. Where the water will come from to frack these wells is a big question that activists and academics are already grappling with. The state legislature is considering bills to put a statewide moratorium on fracking, and environmental groups are girding for a large-scale battle. Colorado River water supplies—which are used by all of Southern California's cities and millions of acres of farmland— will surely be used if and when California moves forward with massive fracking.

Northern Mexico: The Colorado River serves water to the Mexicali region and to northern Baja, Mexico. At this time there is no current or proposed fracking in these regions of Mexico.

So, there's two big take-home messages from all of this, with water quantity and water quality.

Water quantity: Over the next few decades we may see 100,000 new fracked wells in the Colorado River basin or in areas like California and the Front Range of Colorado that are dependent on Colorado River water. With an estimate of up to 4 million gallons of water per well, those new frack jobs would require 400 billion gallons of water. In an average year, the total flow in the entire Colorado River system is more than ten times greater, about 5 trillion gallons of water. But more importantly, given that all of the Colorado River's water is already allocated—the river is drained completely dry before it reaches the Gulf of California, all 5 trillion gallons diverted out—the only way large-scale fracking is going to take place is if some city or farmer that already owns Colorado River water sells their water for fracking. Stated differently, fracking is a new and additional water requirement in a system where there's no water left, and frackers can afford pay practically any price for water and outbid cities or farms when water is for sale.

Water quality: Waste disposal and water pollution are also serious concerns, as depicted by the harbinger in Parachute Creek. With up to two hundred thousand wells, tens-of-thousands of miles of pipes, hundreds of compressor stations and dozens of large-scale processing and refining plants all in Colorado River basin, the chances of spills and accidents are increasing. Disposing of hundreds of billions of gallons of toxic waste in deep injection wells creates unknown risks too—in many ways, the disposal of fracking wastes is much like the disposal of nuclear wastes where government regulators are putting the cancer-causing waste slurry deep underground and hoping it stays there forever. Could just one of these accidents create a large-scale disaster?

When benzene was detected in Parachute Creek about four miles from where the Creek flows into the Colorado River, a spokesperson for the State of Colorado said it was "not a concern" because the increased flow in the Colorado River would dilute the benzene and make the Colorado River water safe to drink. Local citizens were not convinced and complained loudly in the media, and a downstream town on the Colorado River started testing their water for benzene which is extremely difficult to remove from groundwater once the pollution has occurred.

The Colorado River is a very thin lifeline stretching nearly 1,500 miles from Denver to San Diego uniting the entire Southwest U.S.—city, farmer and fracker alike—with one single strand of flowing water. Everything that happens on the landscape across seven states and northern Mexico eventually flows into the Colorado River, and every drop of the Colorado River eventually flows into a city faucet or a farm.
Can we really afford to let the Colorado River get fracked?

--end--

$9 Billion Flaming Gorge Pipeline Would Further Drain the Colorado River System

(*Huffington Post*, January 2012)

Co-authored by Alexandra Cousteau

This'll only cost you
$9 BILLION
StopFlamingGorgePipeline.org

The **Aral Sea** straddles the border of Kazakhstan and Uzbekistan. Two powerful rivers, the Amu Darya and the Syr Darya, feed this inland sea — one of the four largest lakes in the world — and it, in turn, feeds the people and the economy of an entire region. Well... at least it used to.

Under Soviet central planning, the two rivers were deemed more economically valuable if diverted to feed the cotton and rice fields planned for the region by the state. Blueprints were drawn up, dams and pipelines were constructed, and in less than 30 years, one of the great environmental disasters of central planning was etching its mark in salted fields, broken communities, and a sea that is no more. Take a look at these *National Geographic* images — they are shocking reminders of the short-sitedness of trading away the resiliency of an entire region by tapping the very source of the system and draining it to another basin for the sake of short-term growth.

Now, Colorado water officials are proposing to do the same thing in the Southwest United States.

A few months ago, the governor-appointed Colorado Water Conservation Board voted to create a special task force for a proposed pipeline to pull 81 billion gallons of water every year out of the Green River in Southwest Wyoming just before it joins the Colorado River. This week, that task force has its first official meeting.

The proposed pipeline would pump 250,000 acre-feet of water (up to one-fourth of the river's flow) 560 miles across Wyoming, up and over the Continental Divide and down to the suburban sprawl of Colorado's Front Range cities from Pueblo to Colorado Springs to Denver and Fort Collins. At a proposed cost of $9 billion, the Flaming Gorge Pipeline as it is called, would not only create the single most expensive source of water in Colorado, it would further tax the already broken Colorado River system. Already on the brink, the Colorado River is so drained by the demands of California's fields and overwhelming urban growth all across the Southwest U.S. that it no longer runs to the sea. It hasn't done so in almost 13 years now. In fact, the river no longer runs across two entire Mexican states that are now home to its salted and bone-dry riverbed.

If built, the Flaming Gorge Pipeline would irrevocably damage the Green River and further imperil the Colorado River downstream. Endangered fish in the Colorado River basin depend on flows in these rivers. Teetering on the brink of extinction, the Humpback chub, the Colorado pikeminnow, the Razorback sucker, and the Bonytail are listed as endangered by the U.S. Fish and Wildlife Service. But it doesn't just stop with those on the list; the pipeline will also harm wildlife habitat and the recreational economy along these rivers. The Green River below Flaming Gorge Reservoir is a gold-medal trout fishery, attracting fisherman from around the world. The area sports a healthy tourist economy based on rafting and hunting, both of which the pipeline threatens. Communities depend on healthy flows in the river for their financial success. In fact, a group of more than 250 local business leaders has formed to speak out on the issue. Calling itself "Protect the Flows," the group is working to keep water in these rivers so that communities can thrive.

At some point in time, we have to learn from history and say "enough is enough." Trading away the rivers and natural wealth and resiliency of an entire region to fuel the unsustainable sprawl and bluegrass lawns of a few cities is not just foolish, it's morally wrong. We've joined with businesses, communities, West Slope Colorado citizens, and dozens of conservation organizations to oppose the Flaming Gorge Pipeline.

We believe that if the State of Colorado wants to continue to be obsessed with encouraging population growth, it must focus on more sustainable options that benefit the entire region by encouraging smart growth and long-term collaborative management of natural resources. The state has already studied potential water supply alternatives including more aggressive water conservation programs, water reuse and recycling, better growth management, and cooperative relationships with Colorado farmers — these alternatives can and should meet Colorado's future water supply needs.

We agree with the Colorado *Grand Junction Sentinel* newspaper when it **called** the Flaming Gorge Pipeline a "flaming fiasco." Colorado should stop discussing this foolish proposal and seek alternatives that benefit all Colorado River basin people.

--end--

Could the 'Most Powerful Geothermal Reservoirs in the World' Save the Colorado River?

(*EcoWatch*, September 2016)

President Obama made a historic announcement Wednesday, saying that the federal government is considering investing in the geothermal power in the rock formations under the Salton Sea in Southern California. Considered to be "the most powerful geothermal reservoirs in the world," the Salton Sea announcement could play a critical role in the future management of the Colorado River.

Geothermal resources at the Salton Sea.

Fifty years ago, Glen Canyon Dam was built above the Grand Canyon, and the Colorado River was enslaved to generate electricity to feed the hunger of the booming southwestern cities and suburbs. The Colorado's pulsing flows had carved and nourished the Grand Canyon for millennium, but that came to a crashing halt when the gates were closed and the water was ponded in Lake Powell. The environmental damage and steady decline of one of our nation's crown jewels has led to many calls for restoration of the natural system through the removal of Glen Canyon Dam.

The dam's ability to provide power has shielded it from any serious attempt to bring it down. Times change though and, over the last 16 years, the historic drought in the Southwest U.S. has drained Lake Powell to historic lows, severely diminishing the potential to generate hydroelectricity from the massive turbines encased in Glen Canyon Dam. Water and electricity managers are scrambling to come up with a plan to prop up the lake above what's called "power pool" so they can continue to generate and sell power. Any such solution is, however, clearly a stop-gap measure to keep the dam operational and is doomed to fail when confronted by the realities of climate change.

Fortunately, Obama's announcement offers a true path to the future.

The Salton Sea announcement could create an opportunity to replace the hydroelectric power generated at Glen Canyon Dam and a path forward to restoring the Grand Canyon. The geothermal reservoirs under the Salton Sea are an untapped resource that could add power to the grid as Lake Powell is slowly drained and Glen Canyon Dam is removed. Lake Powell's water could be put into Lake Mead, its downstream sister, thus keeping one fully functioning hydroelectric facility on the grid. Further, this "geo-hydro power trade" could keep the federal government solvent in its current financial contracts to provide electricity to the Southwest U.S.

The idea has already generated a bit of a buzz when Geothermal Resources retweeted this tweet:

SaveTheColoradoRiver
@SaveTheColorado

▼ Follow

Salton Sea Geothermal power could be used replace Glen Canyon hydropower as #climatechange drains Powell.#CORiverdesertsun.com/story/news/env…

11:49 AM - 31 Aug 2016

Obama at Lake Tahoe: Big announcements coming on Salto...
The White House will unveil a new agreement on the Salton Sea, and a plan that could spur geothermal development.
desertsun.com

Climate change scientists have painted a bullseye on the Southwest U.S. and the Colorado River, indicating the area will become warmer and dryer with even less flow in the Colorado River. Hydroelectricity is threatened at both Lakes Powell and Mead, as well as reservoirs in California. Salton Sea geothermal power could be a breakthrough in building a climate change-resistant Southwest while also preserving and restoring the lifeblood of the region—the Colorado River.

--end--

Part III: Saving The Cache la Poudre River

Colorado Rivers Illustrate Realities of Extreme Weather Activated by Climate Change

(EcoWatch, September 2013)

The river raced. I was standing near the bridge on College Avenue over the Cache la Poudre River in Fort Collins, CO. Due to the torrential rainstorms, the river had peaked about six hours earlier in the middle of the night, but it was still flowing about 100 times bigger than it usually does in September. A huge tree raged along in the floodwaters, smacked up against the bridge with a cracking sound, and then disappeared under the bridge. Spectators oohed and aahed–a couple dozen of us were watching, mostly because almost everyone in this town of 160,000 people had nothing else to do. The river, which encircles most of the roads leading out of town, rose up and closed down every bridge. We watched and stared and took pictures.

Gary Wockner, on the edge of the Cache la Poudre in Fort Collins, doesn't want to see its water diverted. Photo credit: Hyoung Chang, The Denver Post

The river spoke in ways I never could.

I am an environmental activist. I became a working environmental activist because of this river, the Cache la Poudre. When I moved to Fort Collins 13 years ago with two small children, we bought a house just two blocks away from the river and played and played in the rocks and sand and water along the river, a wonderful activity for kids and for dads too. And so when I heard about a proposal to build a big dam that would drain and destroy the river, my adult friends and I stood up and started taking action. Activism is like that–you dip in

113

your foot, and then your whole body is soon engulfed, and you become activated to protect and defend what you love.

As a part of my work as a river activist, two years ago I was appointed to a Floodplain Working Group for the City of Fort Collins, on which I tried to encourage a group of developers and business people to take flooding seriously and to not build homes and businesses in the Cache la Poudre River's 100-year floodplain. I was not successful, and was voted down 12-1 repeatedly in these meetings. And it got ugly—I was called derogatory names and funders quit funding our organization because I was trying to protect human life and property and protect the river itself. I was "standing in the way of progress." And then the developers started browbeating the City Council, threatening their re-elections. A majority of the Council caved in, including my pathetic City Councilman who I regret supporting and donating $75 for his campaign, leaving Fort Collins with very weak floodplain regulations. I spoke up in those meetings and to the City Council, my passion and intensity rising, as best I could, but they didn't listen.

On that floodplain group, I learned a lot about floods. A "50-year" flood is of moderate size that has a one-in-fifty statistical chance of occurring in any one year; a 100-year flood is much bigger and way more damaging; a 500-year flood can wipe away low-lying towns and cleave a landscape like a butcher's knife. Along the northern Front Range of Colorado—from Boulder to Longmont to Loveland to Fort Collins—this September flood of 2013 ranged between a 50-year and a 500-year flood event depending on which creek or river it raged through.

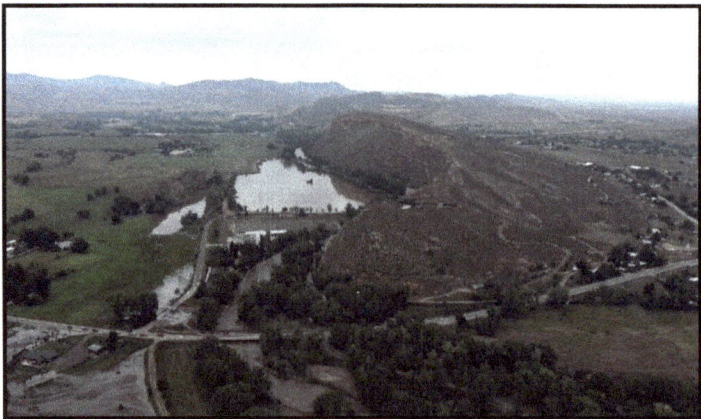

Flooding around the Poudre River in Bellvue, CO, northwest of Fort Collins.

If you were a betting person, you would not have predicted a massive flood in 2013 in Colorado, but with climate change and the new extreme weather it brings, all bets are off. Along the Boulder to Fort Collins mountain landscape, we've had three consecutive years of near-record extreme weather events–near record high snowpack in 2011, near record heat/drought/forest fires in 2012, and now near record high rainfall in 2013.

The forest fires last year in the mountains were huge and damaging in Boulder County but especially the High Park Fire west of Fort Collins in Larimer County. And then this year, the flooding and fires all mixed into a maddening fury when the torrential rain swept over the fire-burned areas. Because the fires killed the trees and charred the soil, the water raced off the landscape carrying with it trees, rocks, mud and coal-black soot which turned the Cache la Poudre River into a black debris-filled torrent. Over the last 12 months, every time it rains the Cache la Poudre River turns black; in this September 2013 flood, the river was a flooding black tornado.

The impacts of the drought, snow, fires and rain are devastating, but the role that politicians play in enabling this chaos is maddeningly worse. As just one example, our Governor, John Hickenlooper (D-CO), has been all over the board on his statements about climate change. He's a former oilman and huge supporter of oil and gas who brags about his oily background and got national media attention when he sat in front of a U.S. Senate Subcommittee and told them he drank Halliburton's fracking fluid. Right before he was sworn into office in 2011, he told the *New York Times* that we should "drill the living daylights out of natural gas" in Colorado, even though natural gas is mostly methane, a greenhouse gas that is an increasingly large contributor to climate change. Those of us in the environmental community who supported him, including me with a personal donation of $1,050 which I wish like hell I could get back now, got snookered. But now the Governor is in an awkward position because he's had to call President Obama twice and ask for federal disaster aid to fight climate-change linked record fires in 2012 and record rain and flooding in 2013. Is the Governor listening yet?

And then there's the oil and gas industry. Every year in Colorado they spend millions of dollars lobbying to make sure that every proposed new regulation is defeated. In Colorado this industry completely controls the state government, donating vast sums of money to the Governor, state legislators and lobbying at the federal, state and local level to gut regulations, increase their profits and further pollute the public's health and our environment. There are 50,000 active oil and gas wells are in Colorado, and over 20,000 in Weld County alone, a county that, as this flood story unfolded, also happens to be downstream and in the path of the raging torrent.

Oil and gas wells toppled in the flood waters

I traveled around the northern Front Range of Colorado during the week of flooding, from Fort Collins to Boulder and Denver, and up and down I-25 corridor through the eastern portion of Weld County. As the rain poured down, the Big Thompson River coming out of Estes Park and Rocky Mountain National Park cut its winding canyon highway into pieces and flooded the city of Loveland down below. This highway is the "Gateway to Rocky Mountain National Park" and may take two years to rebuild which will likely devastate businesses in the city of Estes Park as well as the budget of Rocky Mountain National Park. In years past, I've hiked, skied, camped and watched elk in that park. In the fall, the aspen leaves quake, the elk bugle and the crisp clear mountain air makes you feel that life is pure and natural and never more worth living. Perhaps not this year.

The St. Vrain River to the south, also coming out of Rocky Mountain National Park, shredded the canyon road that ran beside it, marooned hundreds people

116

in the mountains who later had to be helicopter-evacuated, partially destroyed the town of Lyons at the bottom of the canyon and flooded Longmont ten miles east on the plains. Lyons is a small and unique community, with a kayak park on the river right in town, a quaint little main street, and bluesy brew pub that attracts national performers (and me occasionally). It will be years before it is all rebuilt and alive again.

Boulder Creek, even farther south, rose up like almost never before and flooded part of downtown Boulder, air-raid sirens screaming in the night attempting to evacuate thousands of people who live along the Creek's floodplain. Some of the smaller mountain creeks west of Boulder experienced a 500-year flood event. In the past, I've rode thousands of miles on a mountain bike in the pristine canyons above Boulder, including near Jamestown where my first child was born and which was damaged severely in this flood. Most of these canyons are now so covered in mud and debris and pieces of homes and lives that they may never fully physically or emotionally recover.

And then there's Weld County, a few miles east and where the landscape flattens out and where all the creeks and rivers from the mountains flowed into the South Platte River and its wide meandering floodplain. The river rose up and spread across the land as if it had always been there, and knew exactly where to go, covering every nook and cranny—homes, oil wells, cattle feedlots, businesses and highways all submerged and be-damned.

Thousands of oil and gas wells in Weld County were submerged as the river rose. Oil and gas tanks floated along in floodwaters, and oil slicks streaked across the liquid landscape. The State government, which is supposed to regulate the industry and protect the public, has very little manpower and money (due to the endless lobbying by the oil and gas industry) to address this problem. The U.S. Environmental Protection Agency engaged, but also has limited manpower and funding. And so the oil and gas industry—which is worth about a trillion dollars—initially did their own inspections and "self-policed." Using helicopters and boats, the industry shut down nearly 2,000 submerged wells and first reported back to the newspapers that "all's well, nothing to see here, keep moving along." But as the oil slicks increased, the industry changed its tune to say, "yeah, there's a problem, but it's small and we're addressing it." A day later when more chaos unfolded, the industry said, "we're not sure of the exact scope of the problem." And then finally, as the waters receded and a dozen spills made headlines, the industry went into a grotesque public relations spin mode and congratulated themselves for their "heroic actions" that contained the disaster. And then, sickly, Gov. Hickenlooper started parroting the industry's talking points.

For years the industry has fought every new regulation, including those for drilling and fracking beside rivers and in floodplains. Will they ever listen?

Many mountain roads across the northern Front Range suffered severe damage.

Back in Fort Collins, the Cache la Poudre River starts on the northern edge of the continental divide in Rocky Mountain National Park, flows 80 miles down an extraordinary canyon as the only National Wild and Scenic River in the state of Colorado, and then spills on to the plains a few miles west of Fort Collins. In this epic rainstorm event, Fort Collins got lucky because the rainfall along the Poudre River was only about half as much as in Boulder County to the south. As the water subsides, the City of Fort Collins government is surveying the damage, and now gets to decide if it's going to build those new commercial buildings in the floodplain. At one time during our Floodplain Working Group process, the proposed regulations allowed commercial buildings in the 100-year floodplain but required that the business create elevated space inside the building, or roof access, so that when a flood comes, stranded workers (or shoppers) could stand on the roof and wait for evacuation. But, believe it or not, the developers and business people howled and ranted and even got that small regulation removed. And the City will also now decide if it should allow a little subdivision along the river within inches of the 100-year floodplain where, believe it or not, a child could step five feet beyond its driveway and get swept away by the black, muddy, debris-filled torrent. The developer has named the subdivision after a historic name given to the Poudre River, "Pateros Creek." Be careful what you ask for, I said. Will they listen now?

I do this work for a living. I represent environmental organizations and I absolutely love what I do. I travel and speak around the state of Colorado and throughout the Southwest U.S. on issues of river protection, clean water, climate change, drought and now flooding. I speak a lot. I write a lot. I send out a lot of press releases and media updates. I blog, post, tweet. I communicate relentlessly. I also race—with my words, work and life. I try to speak loudly and make a difference.

But most people are not listening, especially the developers, the business people, almost all of the politicians, and of course the oil and gas industry whose short-term profit is the only thought on their mind, and then they buy and sell the elections and politicians to make sure that no long-term planning occurs, to make sure that the long arm of government keeps its business out of their business, until of course a human-caused disaster strikes, then who is the first in line to ask for a government subsidy and bailout?

I speak, write, text, tweet, post, blog, lobby and sometimes I yell.

But nothing I could have ever said, with voice, word, Facebook or Twitter—no press release, no blog, no instagram photo—could speak as well as the rivers did in September of 2013.

The rivers rose up and said, "I am river! Hear me roar!"

Will we listen?

--end--

Will Fracking Destroy Colorado's Rivers?

(*Huffington Post*, March 2012)

Fracking near the South Platte River in Weld County, Colorado.

Oil and gas drilling and fracking pose extraordinary threats to Colorado's Denver metro and Front Range cities including to air quality, water quality in streams and groundwater, wildlife habitat, private property rights, and landscape health. These impacts are generally similar wherever drilling and fracking occurs across the U.S.

But what makes drilling and fracking unique in Colorado — and especially across Colorado's Front Range from Fort Collins to Pueblo — is its threat to Colorado's rivers.

Why? Drilling and fracking use **a lot of water**, and water is already in short supply along the Front Range. In fact, many fast-growing Colorado cities predict they will have a shortage of water in the next decade and are already proposing new water supply projects that will further drain Colorado's already severely degraded rivers. And, the very same cities that are proposing new water projects are also selling increasing amounts of water for fracking.

First, the Windy Gap Firming Project proposes to drain up to an additional **30,000 acre feet** (nearly 10 billion gallons) of water out of the severely degraded Upper Colorado River every year and pipe and pump that water to northern Front Range Colorado cities including Loveland, Longmont, and Greeley. At the very same time, those same three cities have recently started selling water for fracking, and Greeley has started selling large quantities for fracking — over **1,500** acre feet (500 million gallons) in 2011 and climbing. The Upper Colorado already has 60 percent of its water drained out and has severe problems with water quality and water temperature such that fish and aquatic insects are on the brink of survival.

Second, the Northern Integrated Supply Project proposes to drain an additional **40,000 acre feet** (13 billion gallons) per year out of the Cache la Poudre River northwest of Fort Collins. Several towns and cities participating in this project are already selling water for fracking including **Windsor, Fort Lupton, Eaton, Firestone, and the Central Weld County Water District.** Unfortunately, the Cache la Poudre is one of the most endangered rivers in America, already has over **60 percent** of its water drained out before the river reaches downtown Fort Collins, and is sometimes **drained completely dry.**

Third, the Seaman Reservoir Project by the City of Greeley on the North Fork of the Cache la Poudre River proposes to **drain several thousand acre feet of water** out of the North Fork and the mainstem of the Cache la Poudre. Greeley's water sales for fracking, noted above, are escalating.

Fourth, one of the biggest proposed projects in Colorado is the Flaming Gorge Pipeline which could take a massive amount of water — up to **250,000 acre feet** (81 billion gallons) — out of the Green and Colorado River systems every year and pipe and pump that water to the Front Range. One of the proponents for that project was quoted in the *Denver Post* as saying, "If this new water supply helps with the fracking issues, then, without question, we would consider delivering water for the industry." Downstream from this proposed diversion, the Colorado River's health and endangered fish species are already struggling to survive.

Fifth are several to-be-determined water sales for fracking. The City of Denver has opened up **drilling and fracking** on its property at Denver International Airport. It is unclear at this time who is selling water to those drilling and fracking operations, but the City of Denver is also pushing forward with the **Moffat Collection System Project**, a proposal to drain even more water out of the Upper Colorado River and pipe it to Denver. Also, the City of Aurora has **drilling and fracking** moving into its east Denver suburbs, including at the former Lowry Bombing Range surrounding Aurora Reservoir — it is **unclear** where those drillers and frackers will get water but they will need a lot of it. In addition, the City of Thornton is planning to **grow** to the northeast across E-470 into drilling/fracking territory and is at the same time planning to **divert** tens-of-thousands of acre feet of water out of the Cache la Poudre watershed which is 50 miles to the north to slake the thirst of that growth.

And the list goes on and on, from Pueblo to Colorado Springs to the Southern suburbs of Denver as drilling and fracking move into suburban Front Range Colorado near homes and families, but also near city-owned fire hydrants that provide quick, cheap, clean water that has and will be diverted out of Colorado's endangered rivers.

A well pad along the Cache la Poudre River that spilled oil into the river.

So, how much water will fracking take? Like all things with fracking, there are differences of opinion. The industry-funded Colorado Oil and Gas Association estimates that water used for fracking could be **20,000 acre feet** (6.5 billion gallons) per year as wells are sunk in the suburban Front Range. But some environmentalists believe that number **would be higher** as tens-of-thousands of new wells are drilled and fracked, as old wells are re-fracked, and as that water is never returned to the hydrologic cycle because it is too poisoned and polluted for other uses. In addition, efforts in the 2012 Colorado State Legislature to require drillers and frackers to publicly disclose the amount of water they have used have not yet been successful.

Unfortunately, the federal government does not appear to be taking the issue seriously. Recently, the U.S. Bureau of Reclamation released its "Final Environmental Impact Statement" (FEIS) for the Windy Gap Firming Project (noted above) and although several of the project's participating cities are selling water for fracking, the **FEIS does not analyze** nor mention this use of water even after environmentalists have repeatedly requested it. Environmentalists have **requested** similar analyses for the other projects listed above — federal agencies have not yet responded to those requests.

It is true that the state of Colorado contains millions of acre feet of water, and that fracking may only need a **small percentage** of it. But more importantly and to the point, it is also true that fracking is a brand new use of water, and that the brand new amount of water needed for fracking is coming from many of the same cities that are proposing brand new water projects that will further dam, drain, and divert the last streamflows out of Colorado's rivers.

Some people say that fracking may be a small drop in the bucket of Colorado's overall water supplies, but if these water projects go forward, fracking would certainly contribute to being the last drop in the bucket of Colorado's rivers.

--end--

Boulder County should reject NISP

(*Boulder Daily Camera*, May 2012)

"If the gloves don't fit, you must acquit." Johnny Cochran

The Cache la Poudre River is already drained dry at times -- NISP would take even more water out of the river.

Many folks up here in Fort Collins were stunned to read the comment in the *Daily Camera* last Sunday made by the public works director for the City of Lafayette who said, "The NISP project really fits like a glove."

Let me tell you about the Northern Integrated Supply Project (NISP), a project that would further drain the heart and soul out of Fort Collins.

The Cache la Poudre River is already a seriously impacted river -- due to dams and diversions already in place, 60 percent of the river no longer flows through downtown Fort Collins. Sometimes the river is drained bone dry. If NISP is built, another 40 percent of the river will be drained out, leaving less than 1/4 of the river's natural flow coursing through town, which will not only destroy the aquatic life in the river, it will destroy the river's ecological corridor all the way through Fort Collins. This project would be built to further subsidize and fuel unsustainable sprawl and population growth in Boulder County's towns of Erie, Lafayette, and in the Left Hand Water District north of Boulder.

The Poudre just isn't any river flowing through any town -- it's the heart and soul of our community, flowing practically from one end of town to the other. Like Boulder, we have a bike path running all the way through Fort Collins along the Poudre that cost millions of dollars to build. We also have thousands of acres of natural areas and open space alongside the river and the bike path that have been purchased and preserved to protect not just the flow of the river, but also the flow of nature through our community.

And there's no doubt that NISP is a terrible water project. Here's some facts:

- A diverse Fort Collins City Council voted 6-0 to oppose NISP after spending $750,000 to study its impacts.

- The U.S. Environmental Protection Agency said NISP "is not in compliance with the Clean Water Act."

- The State of Colorado Water Quality Control Division denied NISP an early water quality certification.

- NISP would help force the dry-up of up to 123,000 acres of Colorado farms as communities like Lafayette and Erie continue sprawling over Colorado's farmland.

- One of NISP's proposed reservoir sites is on top of fracked oil and gas wells, and several NISP communities are already selling water for fracking.

That's in part why we put together the "Save The Poudre Coalition," which is a unique coalition of 20 regional, statewide, and national environmental groups dedicated to protecting and restoring the Cache la Poudre River. We also formed "Save the Poudre: Poudre Waterkeeper," a new stand-alone nonprofit aligned with Robert F. Kennedy Jr.'s Waterkeeper Alliance to specifically protect the Poudre River. And our primary intent is to stop NISP. We will fight as long and as hard as it takes to stop this river destroying -- and community destroying -- project.

We have also created an alternative to NISP so that towns like Erie and Lafayette can meet their water needs without destroying the Poudre River -- we call this alternative the "Healthy Rivers Alternative." It focuses on water conservation, water recycling, better growth management, and water-sharing agreements with farmers, which are all commonsense options as opposed to continuing to destroy rivers, sprawl across the landscape, and dry up farms.

So here's our message to Boulder County's Lafayette, Erie, and the Left Hand Water District: NISP has been in the permitting process for over 7 years, and there's no end in sight to how long it's going to take or how much it's going to cost.

This glove don't fit. You should quit, because we ain't gonna.

--end--

NISP would destroy Poudre River

(*Fort Collins Coloradoan*, January 2015)

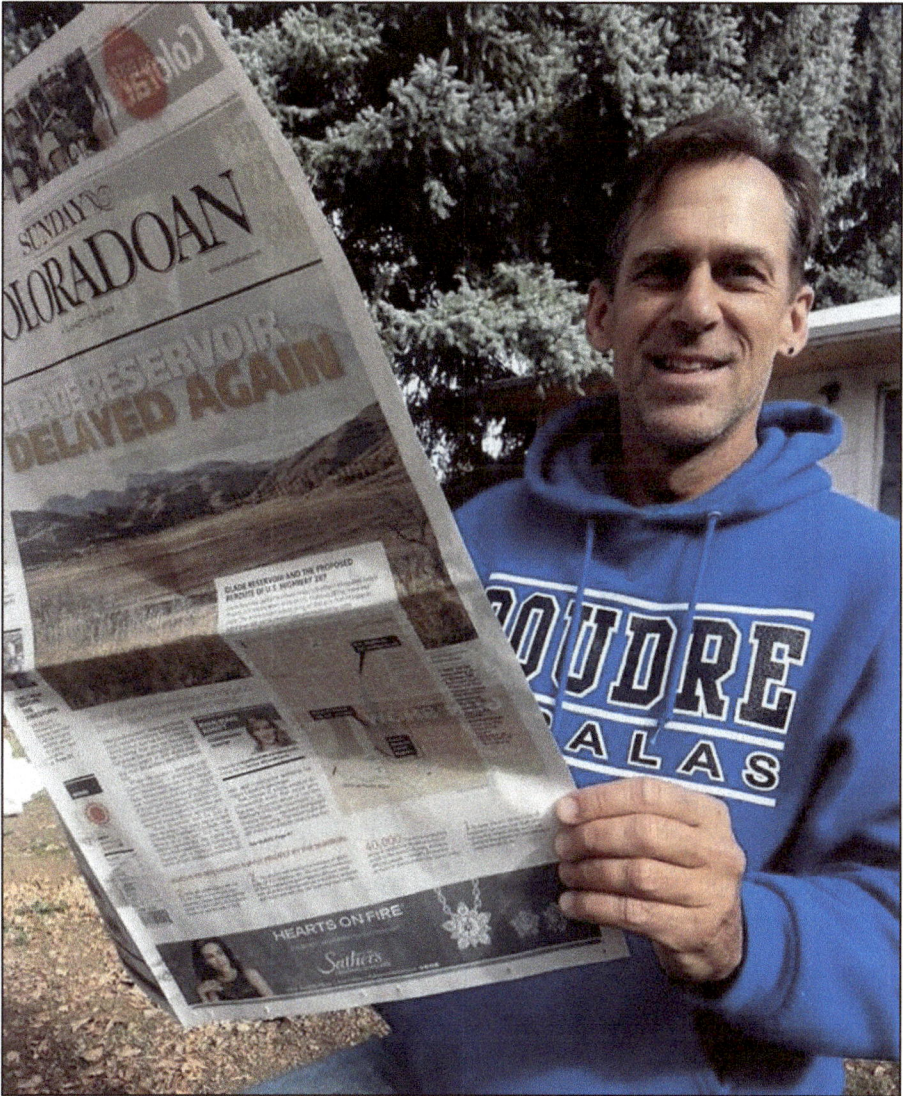

The unending (13 years as of this writing) delays of NISP have been front page fodder for the Fort Collins Coloradoan.

This newspaper's editorial board (Fort Collins Coloradoan) endorsed the Northern Integrated Supply Project in a Sunday editorial that was full of false information and propaganda. Further, the editorial board offered no opportunity for alternative viewpoints to visit with the board.

First, the endorsement talks a lot about Fort Collins, a city that is not involved in NISP. The City of Fort Collins does not participate in NISP, and further in 2008, the Fort Collins City Council voted unanimously to oppose NISP because in part NISP would help kill the Poudre River. All Fort Collins would get is a dry, stinking, muddy riverbed through town if NISP is built.

Second, the endorsement says NISP would protect farms, when nothing could be further from the truth. The growth in Weld County — which is where most NISP water would go — happens directly on top of farms surrounding the small towns that want NISP water. In fact, a technical report released in 2011 indicated that NISP would promote the dry-up and pave-over of up to 123,000 acres of farms in Colorado. The report is titled, "The Farm Facts About NISP," and clearly indicates that NISP would be another nail in the coffin of Northern Colorado farms.

Third, the endorsement completely fails to discuss any alternatives to the project. There are many ways these growing towns can get water, but this endorsement ignores every option other than NISP. The biggest opportunity is to share water with farmers and better manage growth — that way farms could stay in business and NISP towns could get water. Another technical report discusses these alternatives, titled, "A Better Future for the Poudre: Alternative to the Northern Integrated Supply Project."

The biggest problem with this endorsement is that it came out without the Coloradoan editorial board reaching out to opponents of the project. Save The Poudre was not notified the editorial board was discussing NISP, and we were not invited to come in and give an alternative viewpoint.

In years past, Save The Poudre was invited to speak to the editorial board, and as a result the Coloradoan had never before taken a position on NISP.

Here's some more points the editorial board didn't get to hear:

- The United States Environmental Protection Agency said NISP would violate the Clean Water Act.

- Over half of the water in the Poudre River is already drained out before the river gets to downtown Fort Collins.

- NISP would take out as much as 75 percent of what's left of the water out of the Poudre River through Fort Collins in some months and years.

- NISP would take so much water out of the river that it would threaten and drain the proposed multi-million dollar kayak park that voters will vote on in April.

- NISP would further threaten the Preble's Meadow Jumping Mouse, and endangered species protected by the federal government.

- The City of Fort Collins and the City of Greeley both protested NISP because it would dramatically increase flooding through both towns.

- NISP would drain 700 acres of wetlands along the Poudre River, and help dry up and kill the cottonwood forest through town.

The U.S. Army Corps of Engineers has stalled NISP for six years now because the project would have extensive, negative impacts on the Cache la Poudre River through Fort Collins and beyond. Real science must be collected and analyzed because it is required by the National Environmental Policy Act, the Clean Water Act and the Endangered Species Act to ensure the public trust of our shared natural resources.

The citizens of Fort Collins and beyond deserve a healthy and resilient Poudre River, and Save The Poudre will fight as long as it takes to stop NISP keep the Poudre alive.

--end--

LAST STAND ON THE POUDRE

(*Waterkeeper Magazine*, Winter 2010)

You may have heard this quote before, but I'm going to tell it to you again: "In the West, water flows uphill to money."

I repeat this quote to convey a message. I got into this mad fight to save a beautiful river running through my town out of love, out of passion, out of spirit. Many of us—in fact, thousands of us—in Fort Collins and throughout northern Colorado are fighting with everything we have to keep our local river—the Cache la Poudre River—alive. But sometimes the fight seems endless. We have formed the Save the Poudre Coalition, but we haven't saved our river yet. We will, though. We are determined, racing uphill, like water to money in the West.

So here's my message to all of you fighting for a body of water that you refuse to let die: Learn about money. Learn who has the money to destroy your river, and who is making money from its death. Learn how greed combines with political power to ruin rivers. Learn who has the money to pay scientists and engineers to say and write things that are not true about your river. Read the profit statements and examine the budgets of the polluters and dam-builders who are killing your river, and learn about the cost of alternatives to their dams. Study ecological economics and the EPA's new standards on "cost/benefit analyses."

When your river gets dammed, drained or polluted, someone's getting rich. I know. I've watched it happen to our river.

The Cache La Poudre River begins in some of America's wildest lands, high in the peaks of Colorado's Rocky Mountain National Park along the Continental Divide. From there the river rages down the canyons of the Front Range, dropping

7,000 feet as it flows north and east, then spills onto the eastern plains of Colorado, just west of Fort Collins.

Near its pristine beginnings, the rushing Poudre has the protections that come with its designation as Colorado's first and only "National Wild and Scenic River." But as it approaches those plains, it becomes immensely endangered—in 2008, the river conservation organization American Rivers named it one of the "Ten Most Endangered Rivers" in America. Along those last mountainous stretches, three large new dam-and-reservoir projects are being planned. They would cost more than a billion dollars of the public's money and drain the Poudre of its last free-flowing water. This destruction would subsidize and fuel population growth along the northern Front Range of Colorado, and feed the region's addiction to sprawling suburbs surrounded by irrigated bluegrass that doesn't grow naturally with the paltry 15 inches of annual rainfall. But so strong is our addiction to this backyard amenity and other ways of wasting water that even these dams and reservoirs won't be enough.

Temporary rock art in the Cache la Poudre River in downtown Fort Collins

In addition to these threats, two new colossal projects are planned that will suck water out of the Green River and Yampa River—300 miles away— and pipe and pump it up and over the Continental Divide to the sprawling northern Front Range. Because of all of these projects, northern Colorado and the Cache la Poudre River are considered to be ground zero for the next big water war in the West. What happens here on the Cache la Poudre is likely to foreshadow the fate of the many endangered rivers throughout the Intermountain West.

The Poudre is a medium-sized river for the arid West, with an average flow of 300,000 acre-feet per year. As it flows through Fort Collins and onto the plains, about 60 percent of its water has already been sucked out through a massive network of over two dozen ditches, dikes, and dams – 85 percent of that for farms, 15 percent for cities. Here where I live, in downtown Fort Collins, eight miles downstream from the mouth of the last canyon, the river is sometimes drained completely dry – bone dry. By the time the river reaches its confluence with the South Platte, about fifty river-miles to the east, its flow has been almost completely diverted; and even worse, the water that is left in the river is polluted by wastewater plants from Fort Collins and Greeley, and by intense agricultural runoff. This once majestic "Wild and Scenic River" has been turned into a muddy, stinking ditch by journey's end.

Gary Wockner and the Waterkeeper Alliance marched along with 400,000 people in the New York City Climate March.

The folks that want to further dam and destroy our river say that the lower Poudre is a "working river," and that it has to be worked even harder to serve future populations. We say the Poudre has already been worked to death, and we're determined to keep what's left of it alive and begin the even harder work of restoration.

This story would have a nice good-versus-evil spin to it—natural ecological health against the usual portions of human greed and illegality—if it weren't for one major factor: Most of what's being done to the Poudre isn't illegal. The law runs against the river. Water in Colorado, and throughout much of the Southwest, is a legally owned commodity—not a public resource like forests, open space, and wildlife—and almost every drop of water is owned by some entity that has a legal right to use it. This policy, called "beneficial use," stipulates that all water must be used for financial benefit. And further, anyone who owns river water and lets it flow by without using it for financial benefit can lose the right to the water, and someone else can legally take it.

The main impetus for these laws started in the early days of the West's settlement, when water was used in gold and silver mining and for agriculture. Very few people were using Colorado water for pleasure or aesthetic appreciation, and nobody was thinking about the ecological devastation of rivers. So the law stipulated that rights to all the tens of millions of acre-feet of water that flows off Colorado's spectacular snow-capped mountains should be owned and used, and bought and sold like corn and silver on open markets. "Water brokers" and land developers routinely make tens-of millions of dollars as Colorado's rivers—including our Cache la Poudre—are drained dry for cheap water, fast profit and rapid population growth.

This law has changed little over the years, but the West's frontier ethic and the culture it spawned has changed dramatically. Many people in the West now place great value on the ecological integrity of the region's river systems, and derive great pleasure from their rivers. There is also considerable economic benefit tied to that enjoyment. We increasingly recognize that our own well-being is deeply connected to the well-being of the rivers themselves and the myriad species and ecological processes in and around them. We paddle these rivers, build bike paths beside them, fish and wade in them, photograph them, ponder along their banks, or simply watch them.

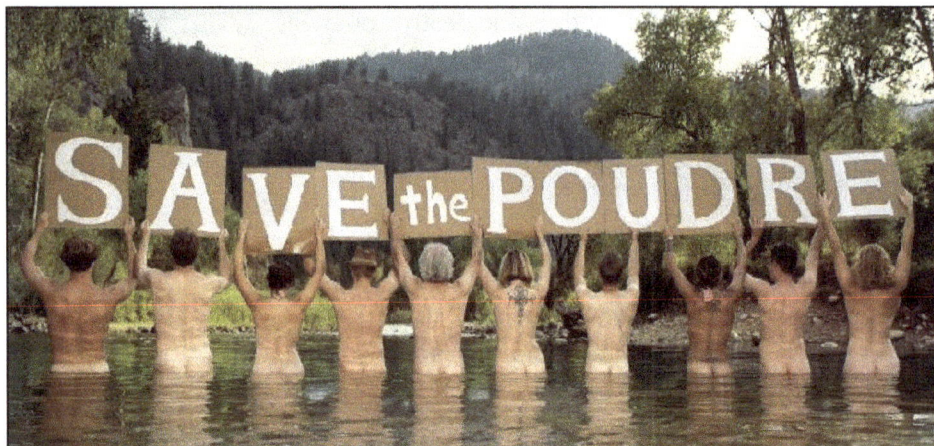

The famous Save The Poudre photo, from New Belgium Brewing.

Yet while the threats to the Poudre continue to grow, so do hope and activism and know-how to save the Poudre. There are many new agricultural-irrigation technologies that could save one third to one-half of the water that is currently used in crop production. And new developments in crop rotation and dry land harvesting and other farming methods could also save water. Residential water use could also be curtailed without the loss of amenities. Drought-resistant landscaping for suburban homes is increasingly available, and myriad low-water residential-irrigation technologies are on the market. Indoor water use could be curtailed with various low-water appliances. In recent years, as more people speak out against water waste, some Colorado leaders have begun to embrace these new landscape aesthetics and technologies, and are beginning to promote government policies and incentive programs that reward water conservation.

Still, it all comes back to money. The dam-and diversion projects on the Poudre have just begun to be scrutinized from an economic standpoint. Money can be spent either to develop more storage through dams and reservoirs—in our case, over a billion dollars worth—or through water conservation rewards and programs, and other related lower-cost alternatives. During the big Western drought of 2002-2003, for example, Fort Collins' municipal government spent $200,000 on a marketing campaign promoting residential water conservation, and the public responded by cutting water use by ten percent. That ten percent amounted to 3,000 acre-feet of water, when one acre-foot was selling for $17,000. That amounts to $51 million worth of water saved by a $200,000 public expenditure—a pretty spectacular return on investment in anyone's book.

Moreover, given the distressed state of the national economy, the State of Colorado and municipalities that want to drain, divert and destroy the Poudre are being forced to re-examine the finances of these projects. Most of the cities and towns (and the developers on their boards and councils) that covet the Poudre's water had hoped to pay for these billion-dollar dams with debt—borrowing the money, then paying it back by charging the cost to new housing growth. But this growth has stalled.

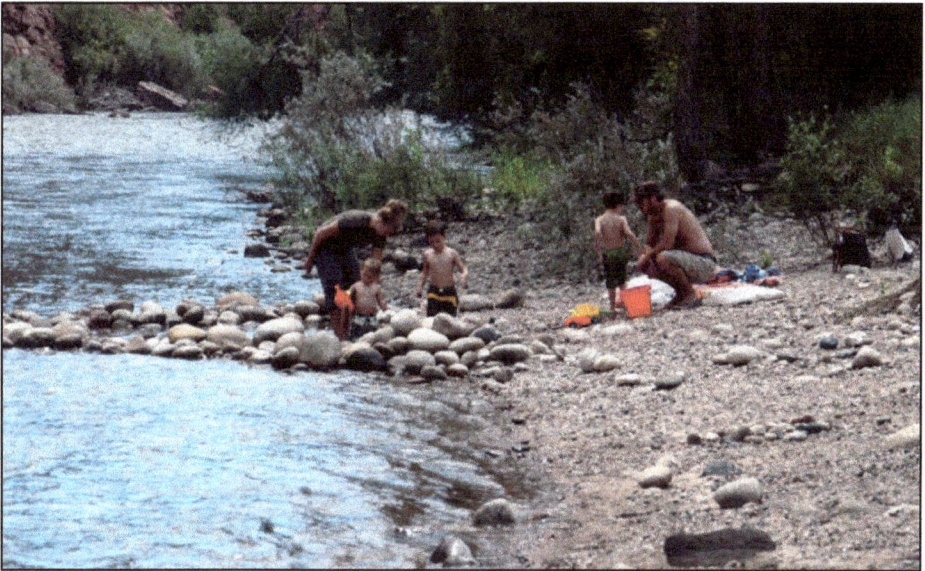

Families play along the Poudre all year.

All of these projects are also subject to environmental impact reviews, involving the National Environmental Policy Act, the Clean Water Act, and the Endangered Species Act, all of which allow for alternative economic analyses to be entered on the public record. The Save The Poudre Coalition has developed an alternative water-supply-and-storage proposal, called the "Healthy Rivers Alternative," that offers towns a way to get the water they need without threatening the lives of rivers or burying northern Colorado in debt. Our alternative proposal is also cheaper and better suits the financial needs of farmers.

Forward-thinking legal efforts are also in the works, such as a new state law in 2009 that will give tax credits to people who own water if they transfer that water back to a river for public ownership. In several counties around the state, small amounts of water have been returned to rivers for fishing, whitewater rafting and kayaking—activities that can be shown to provide financial benefits to surrounding communities and thus legal "beneficial use" of the water. Furthermore, groups around Colorado are starting to create "water trusts"—similar to land trusts—that buy water and keep it in the river for its own health and the people's enjoyment.

A hopeful balance is developing: For every threat posed by the moneyed river-destroyers, there has been an equal and opposite outpouring of love, passion and spirit to keep the Poudre River alive. For example, through the environmental review process, nearly 50 highly trained scientists and lawyers, many of them volunteers, have read thousands of pages of technical reports to help us analyze threats and alternatives. And hundreds of citizens have provided individual comments in the Environmental Impact Statement and have shown up at public events to support the river. Sixteen national, statewide and regional conservation groups, with more than three million members, have joined as "partners" of the Save the Poudre Coalition.

It's true—our love, passion and spirit haven't brought us victory yet. But when we use these inner resources to study the law, to engage the science, and ultimately, to learn about how money kills rivers, we can change the ways that money works. We can, we believe, make water flow downhill, the natural way, to remain where nature placed it, in the magnificent rivers of the American West including our Cache la Poudre.

--end--

Against the Current

(*Pulse of the River*, 2007)

The Cache la Poudre River has many moods -- this one cloudy and wintry. Photo: John Bartholow

The water swirls around her legs and makes little eddies as she walks upstream. I can tell she feels the drag against the current, as if each leg weighs fifty pounds. She leans forward. I love to watch her lean. "Lean," I think to myself. "Move that water. Go where you want." I don't say it out loud, but that's what I'm thinking, what I'm trying to say, though in different words.

I'm in the Cache la Poudre River wading with my eight-year-old daughter, Julia. It's late spring, a Tuesday afternoon, and although flowing like a hurricane up in Poudre Canyon to the west, the river here in town is still nearly dry, its flow diverted by dams, dikes, and ditches before it reaches town. But right here in this one spot just below a little riffle as the river runs nearby our house, the water comes up to Julia's knees and is moving quickly enough to make eddies on the backs of our legs.

I could be at work, but I'm not. Instead, we're looking for crawdads, Julia and I, and we've found dozens. They hide and dart throughout the small rounded rocks on the river bottom. Julia's got a stick and she's poking them out, and then we examine how quickly they swim through the water as they flap their tails backwards. They dart around, always backward, claws facing forward, defensive.

We find all sorts other critters too. Julia points out caddis-fly eggs stuck on the sides and bottoms of several rocks. She's been down here with her school class, and they've studied the river and much of its flora and fauna. Small minnows circle our legs, and one small trout swims in a pool just ten feet downstream. On the banks we see many small trees ringed with beaver cuttings, and we see a few willow trees completely chewed down, their pointed stumps and tendrils circled with the chopping pattern of beaver teeth.

Julia pokes and prods at the crawdads as we wade around. "Dad," she says, her face glowing, "look!" And I do. Or at least I try to. But you know how it is when you're a parent—my mind is in fifty different places and I'm thinking about work, about making dinner, about fixing the porch roof, about the Poudre's politics and activism I'm involved in, and about what the hell to do with my life. But I try to fit in these river escapades with my family because I love the river. I love the way the river makes us all feel.

"Dad," Julia exclaims, pointing, "that one's got a huge pincher arm!" Wow. Indeed it does—it's an inch long, and the crawdad is waving its arm at us like we're perilous predators hell-bent on murder and destruction. Our intentions are more benevolent today, but I wish I did not feel that, at a broader level, the crawdad is right. If it knew what de-watered future could be in store for its habitat, it might then wave that pincher even more aggressively.

As we wade in the river, Julia asks me dozens of question of a biological sort, and I know only a few answers. I enjoy rivers, but I don't study their ecology. Mostly, I just enjoy coming here. Three or four times a week, I have a jogging route that leaves our house, which is a few blocks away, and takes me on a two-mile loop around the river. On some weekdays like today, and on weekends, our family comes down here together.

When we moved to Fort Collins several years back, I looked for a house as near the Poudre as possible. The Poudre flows through town amidst a broad swath of natural areas encompassing thousands of acres and numerous ponds. It is beautiful, and though far from pristine, it offers a natural respite—an escape—amidst the ever-growing metropolitan area of Northern Colorado.

Over the past few years, our family has walked the Poudre's banks, biked and ran along the paved path that runs miles beside it, waded in it, swam in it, chased crawdads in it, and watched wildlife around it. I come down here almost every day for a walk, a run, or some kind of adventure with the kids. I've developed a strong attachment to this river, even a kind of defensiveness. The Poudre's greenness pulls me to it—I don't understand this, I just know that it is true, and always has been. I was raised beside a river, and ever since then I have been pulled to the greenness of rivers, often against the current. Today, Julia and I lean forward, into it.

Summertime fun for kids in the Poudre near downtown Fort Collins.

*

The Cache La Poudre is an extremely threatened river. With its headwaters at the north, west, and southern edges of Larimer County amidst three mountainous forks, the river enjoys relative freedom at its pristine mountain beginnings. But as these forks converge dozens of miles downstream near the mouth of Poudre Canyon, the threats grow immensely. Currently, three new dam-and-reservoir projects are in planning stages near the confluence of the Poudre's forks. In total, these projects will cost over a half-billion dollars of taxpayer money.

The reasons for the Poudre's imminent demise are the usual: ever-growing populations of people (including me and my family) along the Northern Front Range of Colorado, and increasing demands by rural agriculture. These are, in fact, the very same perpetrators that currently use almost all of the Poudre's water and have Julia and me standing in an almost-dry river on this late-spring day. As the Poudre flows out of the canyon and out onto the plains through Fort Collins, about ninety percent of its water is already sucked out in a massive network of over two dozen ditches, dikes, and dams.

Here near my house, which is three miles downstream from the mouth of the canyon, the river is nearly dry about eight months a year. Thirty flat miles farther downstream, where the Poudre meets the South Platte River southeast of Greeley, the Poudre is a mere whisper of its former self—it's once majestic and sparklingly clear flow has been transformed into a fifteen-foot-wide muddy and stinking ditch.

A successful hatch in the wetlands along the Poudre River. Photo: John Bartholow

This story would have a nice good-versus-evil spin to it—the usual bit of illegal human greed versus natural ecological health—if it weren't for one major factor: the law runs against the river. Water in Colorado, and throughout much of the West, is legally a commodity—not a public resource like forests, open space, and wildlife—and every drop of water is more-or-less owned by some entity that has a full legal right to use it. This idea, called "beneficial use," stipulates that water must be used primarily for human financial benefit. And further, if you own that water right and let it flow by in the river without using it for your financial benefit, you can lose your water right and someone else can legally take it.

The main impetus for these laws began back in the early days of the West's colonization when water was used in gold and silver mining operations. At that time, few demands were made on water for agriculture, and Colorado's population was minimal. Further, nobody was thinking about the ecological devastation to rivers, and further yet, very few people were using Colorado water for human enjoyment. The law thus stipulated that water rights should be owned and used, and so every drop of the tens-of-millions-of-acre-feet of water that flows off Colorado's spectacular snow-capped mountains is a legal commodity much like a crop of corn or hillside deposit of silver ore. The right to use Colorado's water is, in fact, bought and sold on open markets somewhat like corn and silver.

Times have changed drastically, but the law has only changed a smidgen. The West's culture, as a whole, is grappling with a new watery vision, one that sees profound uses in functioning ecological river systems and finds incredible enjoyment in rivers. We increasingly recognize that the river itself, and the myriad species and ecological process around the river, serve intrinsic and necessary purposes. We also paddle rivers, build bike paths beside them, fish them, wade them, watch them, photograph them, and write by them. But the law still stipulates for the primacy of human financial "beneficial uses," and the entities that are planning the current dams and diversions on the Poudre—and they include cities, ditch companies, and farmers—still own the water rights and have every legal option to develop and use it.

This kind of schism—where laws and entrenched financial systems lag behind ideas and visions—is at the heart of the West's water chaos. This schism underlies both of the biggest uses of Poudre water—irrigated agriculture, and residential use—and thus the future health of the Poudre remains murky at best.

About eighty percent of the Poudre's water is used to grow irrigated agricultural crops in Larimer County and on the Eastern Colorado plains. Even though irrigated agricultural is an ecological misfit in the West, it has a long history of water rights ownership dating back to just after the mining era, and it has very important political clout through Colorado and the West. A smaller amount of the Poudre's water—roughly ten percent—is used in residential homes and to grow their water-guzzling bluegrass lawns along the Northern Front Range. A green and manicured lawn is a potent symbol of middle-class success, and even though lawns are also profound ecological misfits in the West's dry environments, most homeowners still choose lawns for landscaping.

These two main uses of the Poudre's water offer significant challenges to any effort to restore the river's health. Additionally, future demand on water continues to increase due to expected population growth. Conspiring in this future growth, the various chambers of commerce and economic development commissions of Northern Colorado are spending millions of dollars every year luring ever-more people and businesses to the area.

While these threats continue to grow, it is equally true that a mixture of hope, activism, and technology to save the Poudre is also growing. In the context of irrigated agriculture, many new irrigation technologies exist that could save one-third to one-half of the water that is currently used in crop production. Additionally, newly developed farming methods like crop rotations and dryland crop species could also save water. Ironically, the recent West-wide drought has forced many farmers to consider new irrigation and farming methods, and forced government leaders to begin developing incentives and policies that will allow agricultural producers to sustain their farms with less irrigated water.

Residential water use could also be curtailed without the loss of the public's amenities. Drought-resistant landscaping is increasingly available, and myriad low-water residential irrigation technologies are on the market. Additionally, indoor water use could be curtailed with various low-water appliances. As more people speak out against water waste, some leaders of Northern Colorado cities are beginning to embrace these new landscape aesthetics and technologies, and are beginning to embrace government policies and incentive programs that reward water conservation.

Kids chasing critters in the Poudre River. Photo: John Bartholow

The word, "reward," is likely the key ingredient that will help save the Poudre, because the three dam-and-diversion projects in the works have yet to be scrutinized from an economic standpoint. Money can be spent one of two ways in these water issues: 1) to develop more storage through dams and reservoirs, or 2) through water conservation rewards and programs. During the latest drought, for example, the City of Fort Collins spent only $200,000 on a marketing campaign promoting residential water conservation, and the public responded by cutting water use by ten percent. That ten percent amounted to 3,000 acre-feet of water, and at the time of the drought, one acre-foot of water was selling for $17,000. Thus, the public saved $51,000,000 worth of water by spending $200,000 on a marketing campaign. Myriad rewards and government policies that promote agricultural and residential water conservation could have similar effects. Water can be conserved much more cheaply than it can be impounded behind dams and without any of a dam's ecological costs.

Conserving water, though, will only get us half-way toward a healthier Poudre. Because current water law requires "beneficial use" that forces water owners to "use or lose" the water to another downstream user, those laws will have to be changed before any of that conserved water remains in the river. Fortunately,

Colorado is beginning to address this underlying problem. Forward-thinking legal efforts are in the works that will allow the transfer of ownership of water back to rivers for their ecological health and for human enjoyment. Currently, in several counties around the state, small amounts of water have been transferred back to rivers for the needs of fishing and whitewater rafting and kayaking.

After we have the legal mechanisms in place, what's also needed, and is just beginning to occur, is to create financial mechanisms to buy the rights to water from willing sellers and transfer those rights back to rivers. Just as we have "open space funds," there's no reason why we can't have "river health funds" that buy rights to water at market prices and keep water in the river for the greater good. Already, some forward-thinking individuals, organizations, and cities in Colorado have donated water for instream flow rights in their local rivers, and are considering buying rights to water for whitewater parks and other ecological benefits.

In short, The Cache la Poudre River does not have to die. Many folks are working hard to heal our water schism, and here in Northern Colorado along the Cache la Poudre, we sit at an opportunistic forefront of vision and hope. The Poudre is extremely threatened, but ironically, it may be that very threat—that necessity-as-the-mother-of-invention—that pushes us towards a more healthy river, and healthy life.

When flows are high enough, you can canoe the Poudre through Fort Collins. Photo John Bartholow

*

I have a confession to make: I am extremely biased towards this river. As Julia and I wade in the river and poke at crawdads, I watch a few joggers run by on the dirt paths that surround the river, and this scene reminds me of my own jogging regimen and the reason for my bias.

I went through a "period," you might call it, that lasted ten years where I didn't exercise at all. It was a rough ten years—I was starting a family, launching a career, and we moved around the country too many times. During that "period," I felt like each leg weighed a hundred pounds, like I was continually walking against the current. The sun didn't seem to shine, my vision was cloudy, and my body and mind were ever-more molded around an office chair in a fluorescent-lit room. When I wasn't sitting in an office chair, it seemed I was either shoveling goopy baby food into my daughters' mouths, or shoveling clothes into the washing machine. In the worst moments, it felt like my skin was crawling off my body, and like the neurons in my head were coated with a thick mold.

And so when we moved to Fort Collins and started looking for a more permanent place to live, I was determined to begin anew and find a place to heal my schism. I got out the maps of town and looked for all the green spots, and then I drove and walked around the town's many natural areas. The Poudre's greenness jumped out at me as it coursed through the northern part of the city. We ended up buying a small cheap house that was five minutes away from work, schools, and downtown, and two blocks from the river.

I was determined and inspired, and my healing process began. I started walking along the river for a few months, and then later I tried running. Unfortunately though, my hundred-pound legs continued to linger; my other responsibilities continued to sap too much time and energy. A few months later I tried again, then stopped. And then a few months after that I tried again, and then stopped again. My off-and-on attempts at exercise and healing went on for one year, and then two, and then three. I made very little progress.

And then I remembered what they said, the psychologists and therapists, about the airplane's oxygen mask. They use this metaphor of the airplane losing cabin pressure, and all the oxygen masks falling down from the overhead compartment. They tell you to picture yourself sitting amidst your family on the plane. You are beginning to suffocate; your children are beginning to suffocate.

145

You are faced with a dilemma. Your children are too small to grab the masks, and so you have to decide whether to help your children put on their masks, or to put on your mask first. Should you save your children, or attempt to save yourself?

And here is their answer: In order to save your children, you must put on your own mask first. You must first breathe the fresh oxygen, regain your vision and your strength, and then help your children put on their masks. You can't do anything worthwhile for yourself or your family while your own health suffers. In order to save others, you must first save yourself.

In the fourth year of my healing process, I began anew, though differently. I saved up some money, and then I stepped back from my career and began working one-half time in a lower-responsibility position. And then I started running again. After a few months around my little loop here along the Poudre, my body started looking like its old self. Muscles again appeared, my breathing became stronger, and my legs returned to lightness. Two months later, and I could run farther than my loop, or I could do the loop every day.

A few more months of running around the Poudre and another unexpected change occurred: the sun came out, enthusiasm and optimism returned. Opportunity again knocked, and within another few months I found myself working harder and longer again, but now on new issues of personal passion.

A mink makes its living along the Poudre River in Fort Collins. Photo John Bartholow

And so I am biased towards this river. I have a personal connection to the water around my loop. The more water that's in the river, the better I feel. The less water in the river, the angrier I get and the more I vow to defend and restore the Poudre. I love this river, but it's not a humble soft love. It's a manic running love. It's an angry love. It's a fighting love. It's also an educated and politically astute love. It looks toward long-term vision, and like all good love everywhere, it is relentless.

And I am not the only one. In the seven years I have lived near the Poudre, I have noticed something else: The City, County, and State have spent millions of dollars extending the paved path that runs beside the river, and have also spent millions buying and developing the natural areas around the river. The path now runs over ten miles from almost the mouth of Poudre Canyon all the way out east to I-25 amidst tens-of-thousands of acres of public open space, and this path and open space is used by tens-of-thousands of people every month. Plans are in the works to extend the path all the way to Greeley.

Further, since I've started walking and running this loop, the unofficial dirt paths along the Poudre have widened considerably. Six years ago, these paths used to be just a foot wide, or sometimes they were mere bent-down grassy strips running through the brush. But now, most of the running paths along the Poudre are two-feet wide or more, are beat down to solid dirt, and are etched with runners' shoeprints. Not a run goes by where I don't meet other runners—sometimes a few dozen runners—along the Poudre's banks.

There is a critical irony in all of this: We are planning to dam and drain the Poudre at the very same time we are spending millions of dollars to preserve and enhance the natural areas around it. We are trying to kill what has drawn us here, what sustains us, and what heals us.

And so I will put it this way: the Poudre has many friends, and we are not humble soft people. We are biased, we are defenders and fighters who enjoy running against the current, and we are growing stronger with each lap along the Poudre's willowy banks.

Several years after this story was written, Gary and Julia took a helicopter flight along the Poudre River.

*

As Julia and continue to look for crawdads, a small willow branch floats nearby. One of its ends is pointed like a spear with precise chew marks circling the point. The branch has been chiseled off by one of the many beavers that inhabit the river and nearby ponds. Julia grabs the branch and we examine the chew-marks—they are mesmerizing in their uniformity and depth, and I marvel at the skill and relentlessness required of that job.

"I wanna take this home," Julia says.

"Uh-huh," I say back. Our house is already littered with Julia's river treasures—sticks, rocks, squirrel skeletons, dead crawdads, birds' nests, and all sorts of swamp-things like pond scum and cattails. Julia is one of those kids who brings everything home. Every few months, the stink in her bedroom gets so bad that I have to clean it out and move all of her reeking decaying river treasures outside.

We throw the stick up on the bank for saving, and return our attention to the river bottom. With the sun shining brightly overhead, the river rocks shine back at us like jewels. It's hard to believe they are the same grayish rocks that line the shore. But the water works wonders; its wetness illuminates like finger polish. Julia first learned this a few years back—she'd gather these beautiful wet rocks,

148

but by the time we got home, the rocks had dried and turned a grayish dull hue. Not long after that, she discovered rock polishers, and then a polisher eventually turned in our greenhouse, its 24/7 whirring noise softly piercing the air. And then eventually the small polished rocks covered all the surfaces in our house.

Gary and Julia at Tour de Fat, several years after this story was written.

As an hour goes by, Julia and I turn over rocks, inspect crawdads, chase minnows, pick up beaver cuttings, and watch a great blue heron and a red wing blackbird fly by. A huge mass of turkey vultures circles overhead. The wind lightly flows down the river, and we can catch just a hint of the mountain smell that often flows with it. The Poudre starts up near the continental divide at thirteen-thousand feet of elevation in Rocky Mountain National park, and when the wind's just right, you can smell the ponderosa pine, and even the high-elevation lodgepole pine, all the way down the canyon and here in Fort Collins. The closer my face gets to the water, the more I can smell it, and the better I feel.

A few moments later, when I suggest that it's time to leave, Julia asks me this, "Dad, can we go over to McMurray Pond?" She's referring to a five-acre pond about a hundred yards upstream. We often go there with the canoe and paddle around, or we swim or watch wildlife. Once, a year ago, we watched a mother and kitten beaver swim circles in the pond as we paddled nearby.

I think for a second about all the other things I ought to be doing. And then I answer, "Sure we can, Julia."

She asks, "Can we walk all the way in the river?"

I pause, and then shoot back, "You bet."

And then we walk upstream, against the current, and I see her lean forward, into it.

"Lean," I think to myself. "Move those legs. That's the way to get where you want. That's the only way change ever happens."

--end--

A New Water Economy

(*Denver Post*, February 2009)

"Constant dripping hollows out a stone." — Lucretius

The Poudre River smack dab in downtown Fort Collins, drained dry.

The water in Colorado's Cache la Poudre River alone — 300,000 acre-feet — is worth billions of dollars. And the state's biggest river (the Colorado) produces *30 times more water* than the Poudre.

So as we look for the next big thing in economic opportunity, green jobs, and research and development, we ought to look at a "New Water Economy" similar to that of the New Energy Economy.

Water is, after all, a renewable resource.

Gov. Bill Ritter was in Fort Collins a few weeks ago introducing his Senate nominee, Michael Bennet, and discussing the dismal state of the state. As they both spoke, members of the audience were waving signs that said "Stop Glade Reservoir! Save the Poudre River!"

While Bennet and Ritter acknowledged the protesters and the controversial dam-and-reservoir project, they redirected their focus to Colorado's New Energy Economy. That's a term every American environmental group has also picked up, and all for good reason: Investing in clean energy could clear the air, cool the planet, and refuel and rebuild our economy. Colorado is well-positioned to lead in the New Energy Economy; we have ready supplies of wind, sun and a progressive citizenry that wants to push this agenda forward.

But what Colorado has more of than any other Western state is water. We're the King of Water; it's our No. 1 export "crop" in both quantity and dollars. The majority of southwestern U.S. water lands in Colorado as snow and then melts, quenching the thirst and (through farming) eventually the hunger of tens of millions of Americans, from the burbs of Phoenix to the Los Angeles basin. In addition, it helps California farmers grow crops for the entire nation.

In Fort Collins, Ritter and Bennet spoke just 100 yards away from the Cache la Poudre River, a mere mid-sized Colorado river that supports billions of dollars in tourism, recreation and agricultural economies.

Many cities around Colorado are moving forward with water conservation and efficiency programs as a response to drought, the rising cost of water, and as a means to address the new demand for water from population growth. Stated differently, there's a massive government expenditure about to take place around a very expensive commodity that, like energy, every single person needs every single day. We should be using this enormous resource — water and the money behind it — to expand our economy and to create green jobs, protect the environment, and save money.

Water conservation and efficiency programs at the city, state and federal level should be tied to economic recovery and stimulus programs that:

• **Incentivize the private sector to create green Colorado jobs.** Landscaping, landscape architecture, and the nursery industry represent a $1.8 billion economy in Colorado — using government incentives to point that industry in a more sustainable low-water direction would stimulate the economy and put Coloradans back to work.

• **Invest in clean, green Colorado agriculture.** Efficient agricultural irrigation systems are the wave of the future for Colorado's $1.6 billion irrigated agricultural economy. Government expenditures should lead that wave through incentives and investments.

• **Support research and development.** Private industries and Colorado's universities should be prime recipients of grant money to investigate and create new water efficiency technology for residences and agriculture.

• **Save money.** Conservation and efficiency are much cheaper alternatives to wasting massive amounts of money on new dams and reservoirs. Investing in conservation and efficiency can offset future water demand and dramatically minimize public debt, a necessity in this depressed economy.

Here's an example of how a change in public policy could stimulate a New Water Economy: In 2008, Boulder County passed a ballot initiative that allowed homeowners to borrow money from the county to put solar panels on their roofs. This initiative saves energy, saves money by decreasing energy costs, increases the value of the home, and creates jobs in the solar industry.

A very similar change in policy could work for the New Water Economy by allowing homeowners to borrow public money to install high-efficiency irrigation systems or retrofit their lawns with Xeriscaped landscapes. By doing so, water will be saved, money will be saved, the value of the home will increase, and jobs will be created in the high-tech irrigation and Xeriscape sector.

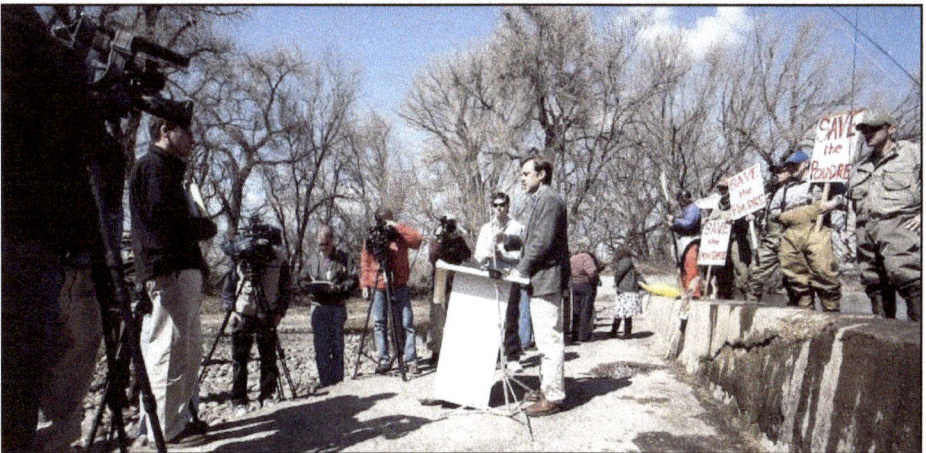

In 2008, the Poudre was named one of the "Most Endangered Rivers in America."

Beyond the needs of the cities, the opportunities in Colorado's agricultural economy are 10 times greater. Ninety percent of Colorado water is drained from rivers and used to grow crops, much of that very inefficiently. In fact, in the Poudre River basin, the river is often drained completely to irrigate crops with what is called "flood irrigation," where a field is completely flooded and the wasted water flows off in large ditches. Government investments and incentives that encourage efficient sprinkler irrigation would save water and thus money, increase the value of farms, and help keep Colorado's rivers alive.

During his visit to Fort Collins, Sen. Bennet said "he'd like to help solve controversial regional issues like the Glade Reservoir project." The New Water Economy could do just that. By investing in water conservation and efficiency and by keeping water in rivers, we will be making a permanent investment in one of Colorado's biggest economic drivers: the natural environment that brought most of us here in the first place.

Case in point: While Ritter and Bennet spoke while standing near the Cache la Poudre River, condos and lofts are popping up nearby as citizens increasingly are drawn to the beautiful swath of open space along the river that meanders through town. In fact, the closer you get to the river, the higher housing prices get. This (and many other concerns) prompted the Fort Collins City Council last year to vote unanimously against the Glade Reservoir project, saying the Poudre was one of the city's "economic engines" that we could not afford to lose.

A New Water Economy, indeed.

--end--

A River Runs Through It

(*Denver Post*, April 2006)

"The frog does not drink up the pond in which he lives." -- Sioux proverb

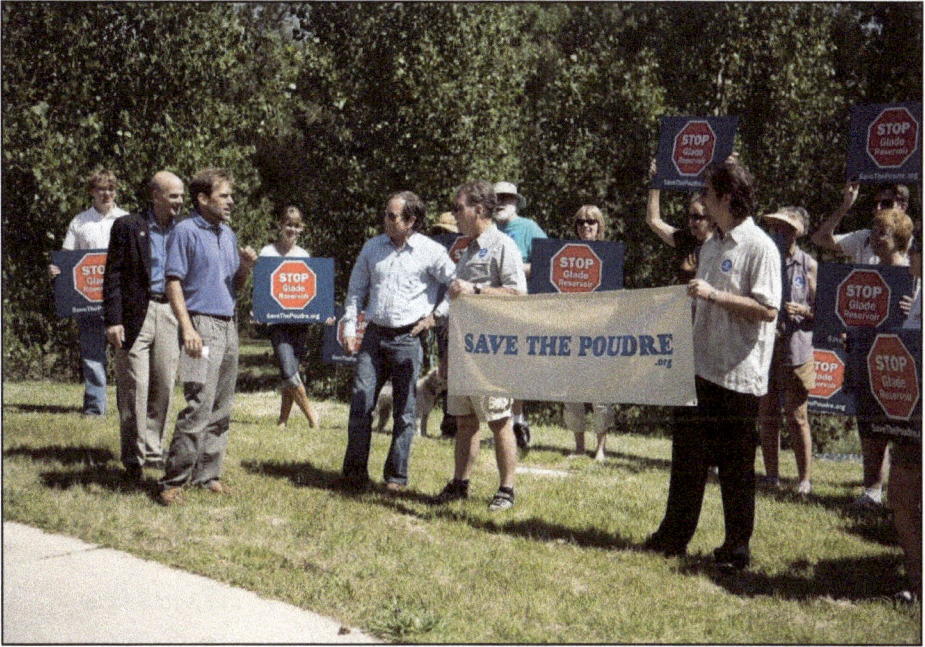

Rallying for the Poudre with elected officials and environmental leaders.

Fort Collins has a river running through it. It's a fine river -- what's left of it -- and I see it almost every day as I walk or jog beside it near my house.

On my outings, I also see wildlife, kayakers, fishermen, children playing and mothers pushing baby joggers. We are lucky here because the city, county, state, various land trusts and GOCO have spent hundreds of millions of dollars building a miles-long paved path beside this river and buying thousands of acres of recreational open space along the shores of its tributaries.

When I first visited Fort Collins and thought of moving here, I walked down to the river -- the Cache la Poudre -- and dipped my feet into its cold, clear water. It was late spring, and the Poudre was boiling with rapids. For me, it was love at first sight. The Poudre smelled good, looked good, felt good. There's nothing like a beautiful river. There's nothing like clean, fast-moving water to put lady luck on your side. I said, "Let's give it try," and I moved my family to town.

Our luck may soon run out.

Recently, several Northern Colorado cities and water districts have proposed three huge dam-and-reservoir projects on the Cache la Poudre. These projects will cost about $750 million of taxpayer money and include the Glade, Seaman and Halligan reservoirs. Proponents of these projects claim they are needed to provide "drought protection" and to "meet the demands of new growth."

These new dams and reservoirs raise four important questions:

First, fiscal responsibility -- Economic analyses often show that using water efficiently and ensuring comprehensive water conservation can provide drought protection, meet growth's demands and not impact "quality of life," all at a lower cost than building new dams.

For example, in 2002 during the peak of the drought, the city of Fort Collins spent $150,000 marketing water conservation. Citizens responded by conserving 3,000 acre-feet of water, 10 percent of annual use. Thus, it cost $50 per acre-foot to save that 3,000 acre-feet of water. Put in context, the new dams will cost between $2,000 and $10,000 per acre-foot, and buying water on the open market will cost between $15,000 and $30,000 per acre-foot.

Quixotically, the city cut that cost-saving program in 2003. In contrast, progressive cities like Boulder conserve about a third of their water by spending up to $450,000 per year on conservation programs.

Second, environmental impacts -- Fort Collins and Larimer County rivers, natural areas and ecosystems will be profoundly impacted by these proposed new dams and reservoirs. Two geographic areas are of specific concern: the Laramie Foothills north of Fort Collins, including the North Fork of the Poudre River, and the main Poudre River corridor running through Fort Collins to Greeley, where it meets the South Platte.

The Laramie Foothills project is a joint public-private conservation effort already conserving tens of thousands of acres, some of which will be flooded, and more of which will be degraded by massive water diversions out of the North Fork. All three reservoirs are smack-dab in the middle of these open-space efforts.

Impacts to the Poudre River corridor would be equally devastating. This corridor includes a unique and much-loved ecosystem supporting wildlife and some rare and endangered species. Currently, more than two dozen diversions suck out at least 80 percent of the Poudre's flow before it reaches the South Platte. At the confluence, the Poudre is but a mere whisper of its former self; its once majestic and sparklingly clear flow has been transformed into an ephemeral, 15-foot-wide muddy and stinking ditch. These new dams will mean even less water for the river.

A small dam removal project along the Poudre that Save The Poudre helped instigate. Photo: John Bartholow

Third, rapid population growth -- Most of the cities proposing to build these projects already have severe budget shortfalls yet are proposing huge debt loads for new dams. This is a formula for bankruptcy or for rapid population growth. The town of Erie, for example, proposes to go more than $60 million into debt for its share in Glade Reservoir, which is about $20,000 for every family in town.

If a city has a budget crisis and it issues bonds to pay for new dams, then it must have fast growth to bring in new development fees and revenues in order to pay off those bonds. Already, a few cities have dropped out of the projects, worrying that they cannot grow fast enough to pay off the debt. In any case, growth intensifies, citizens foot the bill, and the river suffers.

Fourth, economic sustainability -- Tens of thousands of citizens and tourists, including whitewater enthusiasts, fishermen, bicyclists, hikers and recreating families use the Poudre River and our natural areas every year. These people provide a large economic stimulus to northern Colorado's increasingly tourist-based economy.

The huge, recent recreational open-space acquisitions lie exactly in the zone of impact. The Laramie Foothills project is a centerpiece of Colorado conservation, about which GOCO's executive director recently said, "This project is a great example of the landscape-scale protection the GOCO Board intended with its recent Legacy grants."

Likewise, the Poudre River Trail as it runs through Fort Collins and Greeley is an urban recreational resource used by thousands of Larimer and Weld County citizens every day.

--*

Back when I first moved to Fort Collins, I was once stuck in a traffic jam atop the bridge on College Avenue that passes over the Poudre. My youngest daughter, then 3 years old, was fussing in the back seat, so I reached back to tickle her cheek. The Poudre caught my eye. It was June and the river was raging through town. I turned to my wife and said, "My God, that's a wild thing."

Summer fun on the Poudre in downtown Fort Collins.

Soon thereafter, we bought a house a few blocks from the Poudre, and ever since we've used the river and the trail almost every day. We walk, bike, swim, chase crawdads, watch beavers, canoe, skip rocks and build sand castles. My children are now old enough to go down to the river by themselves where they explore, climb trees and wade through swamps.

So, as I began to learn more about the Poudre's imminent demise, I naturally became quite concerned. I talked to friends and their friends, and found out that many, many people were equally upset. Efforts to preserve the Poudre have been ongoing for decades -- the current dam proposals are mere ghosts of past proposals, now popping up in different side-canyons along its meandering tributaries.

While the Poudre's flow may be diminishing, new efforts to preserve the river are strengthening rapidly. Over the past year, a large coalition of Colorado conservation groups has formed to address the threats. This coalition is not "anti-growth" and is certainly not naïve.

We all recognize that demand for water is increasing along with population growth, and we recognize that a broad public dialogue is needed to ensure our area's economic and environmental sustainability.

This coalition is working on several new ideas about water conservation and efficiency, entering into legal agreements with farmers to buy/lease/share water and retiming the flows in the Poudre for conservation purposes.

The coalition is also interested in not just preserving the Poudre but in restoring historic streamflows. We are discussing conservation strategies that involve free-market incentives, and in connecting with a "water trust" -- an entity that would buy/lease/share water for conservation purposes.

The water trust movement is just beginning in Colorado and is poised to be the next big thing, much like the land trust movement was 30 years ago.

Ultimately, the coalition seeks a balanced approach to preserving our unique quality of life. Here in northern Colorado, we have a wonderful river with a curiously wonderful and unique name -- the Cache la Poudre. The Poudre is a true wild thing in a world in which wildness is increasingly rare. A balanced approach will make sure Fort Collins always has a river running through it and that our citizens are always lucky to enjoy it.
--end--

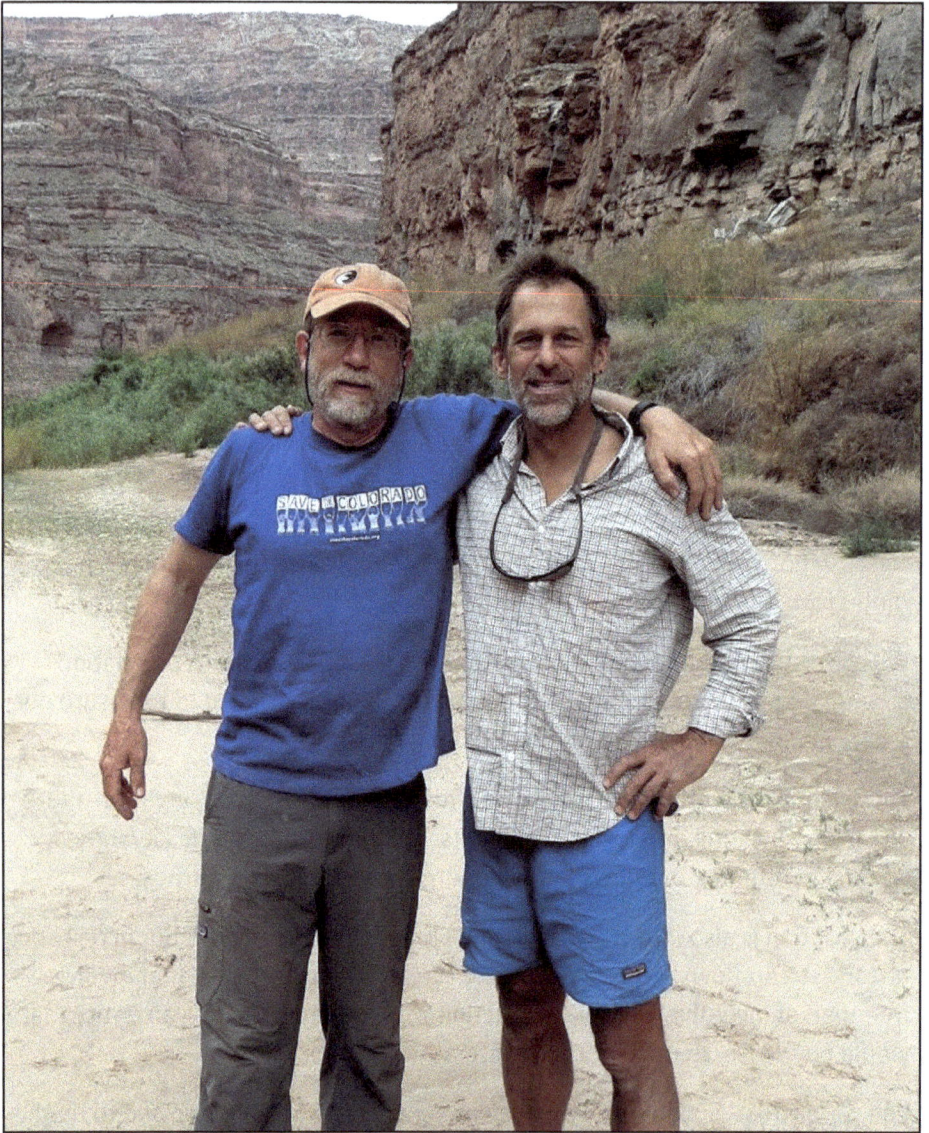

Mark Easter and Gary Wockner (2016), along the Colorado River. Mark co-founded Save The Poudre and serves on the board of both Save The Poudre and Save The Colorado.